# TEN STEPS TO
# Finding
# HAPPY

## A guide to permanent satisfaction

Selene Castrovilla
Lindsay S. Weisner, Psy.D.

Books published by Last Syllable Books are available at special discounts for bulk purchases in the United States by corporations, institutions, and other organizations. For more information, please contact Independent Publishers Group: 1 (800) 888 - IPG1 or email @ipgbook.com

Castrovilla, Selene & Weisner, Lindsay S. Psy. D.

Ten steps to finding happy: a guide to permanent satisfaction/ Selene Castrovilla & Lindsay S. Weisner, Psy. D. – 1st ed.

Design by Damonza

Ten Steps Illustrations by Reem Abi Samra

Ask the Experts, From the Doctor's Desk & Selene's Story Graphics by Meredith Samuelson

Includes bibliographical references.

ISBN: 978-0-9964306-6-1          E-book ISBN 978-0-9964306-7-8

Library of Congress Control Number: 2019910046

1. Happiness Self-Help.. 2. Motivational Self-Help. 3. Personal Transformation Self-Help 4. Emotions & Mental Health. 5. Emotional Mental Health. 6.Self-Esteem. 7. Cognitive Psychology. 8. Healing. 9. Happiness. 10. Mid-Life Management.

*For my son, Michael*
*Who challenged me to write this book with the deadline of his*
*birthday—and who makes me happy!*
*Happy birthday and happy every day, Michael.*

—Selene Castrovilla

*This book would not have been possible without the love, support,*
*and never-ending patience of my husband, Scott. My laptop became*
*a shiny new attached appendage for six months, and during that*
*time he never judged, never criticized, and even managed to teach*
*our eight-year-old daughter to roller skate while I typed. Thank you*
*to my two children, Hunter and Elexis, for their kindness, love, and*
*support for their distracted Mommy who still fails to appreciate the*
*importance of Pokemon Cards. Thank you to my parents, my family,*
*and my friends for the enthusiasm that prevailed long after my own*
*had begun to wane. Thank you to our expert contributors who we*
*somehow, magically, persuaded to give us their time, their words,*
*and their wisdom, so that we could, in turn, give it to others.*

—Lindsay S. Weisner, Psy.D.

Expert Contributors:

*Dominique Andriese, Alexa Carlin, Nina Chmiel, Dr. Niloo Dardashti,*
*Alexandra Farbenblum, Casey Lee Ferri, Nicole Glassman, Max*
*Grey, Peter Grossman, Candice Hoyes, Dr. Alisa Hurwitz, Daniel*
*Lamas, Nicole Lee, Sandee Leonhard, David Mahler, Dr. Erin*
*O'Callaghan, Elora Philbrick, Orel Protopopescu, Brian Reinthaler,*
*Meredith Samuelson, Sharone Sapir, Beth Star, Sarah Temech,*
*Dr. Scott Weisner, J.D.*

# CONTENTS

# INTRODUCTION

Ah, happiness. Our search for it is universal, timeless, and endless. War, politics, and religion have brainwashed us into believing that we should focus on our differences.

We say, let's embrace what we have in common.

We are all human, sharing a planet and trying to get by.

We are all looking for happy.

*"The most important thing is to enjoy your life—to be happy—it's all that matters."*

—Audrey Hepburn

So why do we think that finding happy is so difficult?

It's not—sort of.

Like anything important and worthwhile, finding happy is a process and a journey. This is actually a gift: You only appreciate what you have to work for.

Like a college student who procrastinates writing a paper on *Wuthering Heights*, we put off finding happy. Instead, we look for a quick fix—reading the CliffsNotes, or watching the movie. Perhaps we hire someone else to do the work, or we plagiarize the work someone else has done. But we are hurting ourselves when we do this—inflicting deep, scarring wounds.

There is no shortcut, and the beauty of finding happiness is actually in the effort. You can enjoy the journey—and even the hard work. And when you realize you're not alone, life is a lot less terrifying.

You already know what to do to find your own happiness. You know the way. What we will show you in this book isn't some ancient secret of the sphinx. But so far in life, you've done everything you can to avoid doing the coursework.

*"All know the way; few actually walk it."*

—*Bodhidharma*

Instead, here you are, hanging out in your dorm room with a "Hang In There!" poster of a cat peeling off the wall, getting wasted and wishing your life were different.

Yes, you've been wasting your life, fooling yourself into believing you're lost.

We are here to remind you of the way—and to guide you.

*"The journey of a thousand miles begins with a single step."*

—*Lao Tzu*

We are all in the college called life, and it's up to each of us to fulfill the requirements and graduate into happy. The trick is that it's a one-person major— each of us has our own unique requirements. The steps, or "courses", are the same for everyone, but how you complete them is unique. Let's call this the "snowflake effect." Just as no two snowflakes are alike, so are no two people. So how could you find your happy in exactly the same way?

What moves you?

Is it a beautiful sunset? That one sad song that reminds you of the loss of your first love? The picture from the last time you saw your grandmother?

What affects you?

Does the latest report on the poverty level in America stress you out for days? Do you pore over Instagram posts looking for the latest surefire, scientific revelation on the food that will make you taller, younger, or smarter?

Generally speaking, the left side of our brain controls logical thoughts, language, and numbers. The right side of the brain controls emotions, spatial information, and visual comprehension. In reality, the whole right brain/left brain idea is an oversimplification. But it is true that some people are more drawn to a more logical reasoning while others thrive in the beauty of emotions.

With that in mind, we have structured this book in a way that we hope appeals to all of our readers, both those who meticulously go over their bank statements and those who toss money into their account when the balance seems low and hope it all works out.

Our goal from the beginning has been to write a book that offers you ten steps to finding your happy, along with a selection of solid, simple Concrete Actions for following through with those steps. We won't leave you hanging, wondering what to do!

Selene Castrovilla tackles the emotional perspective, peppered with personal anecdotes and honest admissions.

In the sections titled *From the Doctor's Desk*, Dr. Lindsay S. Weisner offers logical, research-based, psychologist-approved information that will provide the PROOF for which lovers of reason thirst.

Read both, and figure out what moves you more, your mind or your heart. There is no right or wrong answer.

BONUS! In the *A Note From the Expert* segments, guest writers deep dive into their professions, providing clear information and scientific evidence backing up our ten-step process.

We have you covered.

In this book, you can choose to follow your head or your heart to your future happiness.

Enjoy!
Selene Castrovilla & Dr. Lindsay S. Weisner

*"Be yourself. Everyone else is already taken."*

—*Oscar Wilde*

FROM THE DOCTOR'S DESK:
LINDSAY S. WEISNER, PSY.D.

We want you to step up to the plate and be accountable for your actions. We want you to live a life that is more active and less passive. We want you to decide that you want to be happy and be willing to break free from your comfort zone in an attempt to reach that happiness.

However, there are times that our feelings of sadness, hopelessness, and helplessness can feel overwhelming. If your unhappiness leads you to thoughts of harming yourself or others, your first step is to keep yourself safe by calling 911 or going to the nearest emergency room.

Please remember to take care of yourself first.

When you are feeling better, our steps will be here for you.

# So what, exactly, are concrete actions

Concrete actions are daily activities that provide a fast and direct route to a happier you. No waiting, no thinking, just simple actions you can take immediately to make you happier. Utilizing them can help you find your footing in the ten steps we have laid out for you.

Some of these concrete actions are things you may already do, like listen to music. Others may seem silly, even childlike. But there is a method to our attempts to unwind you from your feelings of madness or sadness. Did you know that people who try a wider variety of activities are more likely to remember positive experiences and minimize negative experiences? There is even a part in the brain that scientists refer to as the "novelty center." This is the part of the brain that lights up when you try new things—it doesn't matter if you end up liking or hating the new thing, either! And those lights? They are actually hormone surges. Your body and brain flip the happy switch when you try new things. Keep an open mind and try out as many concrete actions as you can!

Lastly, Dr. Weisner and I urge you to take a moment at the end of each step to celebrate your accomplishment! It can be in any way that appeals to you—even as simple as a smile. The self-acknowledgment is what counts.

## Concrete Action

# Go Shopping

*"I keep threatening to keep a formal journal, but whenever I start one it instantly becomes an exercise in self-consciousness. Instead of a journal I manage to have dozens of notebooks with bits and pieces of stories, poems, and notes. Almost every thing I do has its beginning in a notebook of some sort, usually written on a bus or train."*

—Walter Dean Myers

Buy yourself a notebook or journal.

Yes, technology has taken over the universe and handwriting seems old-fashioned and antiquated.

But in this case, keeping notes on your smart phone just won't cut it.

The act of putting pen to paper gives you more freedom than typing (or texting). When you write, you engage in an unconscious creative process—one that you may not even be aware of. When you write by hand you make decisions about how to present information in a way that will be memorable to you. Perhaps you write larger for more important points or draw bright red exclamation marks over the things that surprise you.

Note-taking by hand allows you to be the artist of your internal processing. Do you write in script? What color do you write in? Your subconscious may guide you, and you won't even notice.

As adults, handwriting is a simple, automatic task. The simplicity of this process paves the way for a stream of consciousness experience. Stream of consciousness is just a random word association, a sometimes-rambling, sometimes-confusing verbal vomit of your thoughts and feelings.

Typing—or texting—requires you to consciously tap into the part of your brain that holds the technical stuff. In the process, an unconscious self-editing may happen. In other words, you may not express yourself as freely as you would by hand. There may be other advantages to taking notes by hand as well, as some research suggests that hand-written notes may lead to a better understanding of the material.

And in this case, a better understanding of yourself means a better understanding of how to find your happiness.

Treat yourself with a brand-new notebook or journal that appeals to you. This is your special place for recording your thoughts and feelings as you complete your concrete actions. Sometimes we pose questions you might want to reflect on, and sometimes the steps might trigger your own thoughts you want to record and remember. Don't forget to choose a cool pen in a color that speaks to you.

Purple is said to connect us with our deeper thoughts and inspire high ideals. Green is the color of growth, harmony, and balance. Orange is associated with enthusiasm and determination.

Or, you may choose to write notes inside this book and highlight what you find especially important. (Assuming it's not a library book!)

Of course, you can do both!

### Selene's Story

I have bought fancy, gorgeous journals—but every time, I freeze with my hand poised, facing the prospect of what I could possibly write inside that would be worthy of such an elegant and expensive binding! And it would have to be perfect. And neat! I scrawl, nearly illegibly—sometimes it is truly illegible, and I have to guess at what I meant, which can be fun and leads to further thoughts—and what could possibly come out perfect? The process of writing lies in rewriting!

So, I most often enjoy the simple marble composition notebooks. They're cheap enough that I can start a new one for a different topic, on a whim, without any guilt. They come in different colors—I love purple, and that's what I use, modifying only in shades. I buy a stack of them when they're on sale (at back-to-school time, usually). Sometimes I find them in the dollar store. Such pleasure for a buck! Beats the heck out of candy, which is a temporary high. Sometimes the notebooks have different designs on them, but I always stick with purple. It's my thing.

Dr. Weisner and I encourage you to find your "notebook thing." It seems little, but the little things add up to a lot.

Sometimes satisfaction lies in life's little details.

*"It has long been an axiom of mine that the little things are infinitely the most important."*

—Sir Arthur Conan Doyle,
"A Case of Identity"

And as for the big things? Maybe they're just a compilation of all the little things.

*"Great things are done by a series of small things brought together."*

—Vincent Van Gogh

# CHOOSE TO FIND HAPPY

*"Most folks are about as happy as they make up their minds to be."*

—Abraham Lincoln

his sounds simple, doesn't it? Too simple, perhaps, because it tricks us. Sure, we can say, "I choose to find happy."

Hurray! Step one done!

Not so fast. Because although choosing to find happy is easy, it certainly isn't simple.

We have to actually believe what we say. We need to cradle the pursuit of happiness inside our heads and our hearts every day. And sometimes, in order to get us out of our rut—and to get ourselves out of our own way—we have to introduce something new in our lives. Or something old that should be new again. Remember hopscotch? How fun was that? And what would that be like to try that again now....

*"Change your thoughts and you change your world."*

—Norman Vincent Peale

So how do you actually set your mind—and your heart—on finding happy?

---

## Concrete Action

# Sign a contract with yourself

This contract is your invitation to be accountable to yourself.

Don't worry, you don't need to hire a lawyer or find a notary. Just fill it out and sign it. And celebrate it! Make this moment fun and important! If you're feeling artsy, decorate the contract with colors that inspire you or memes that make you smile. If you're a religious or spiritual person, write a letter to God or the universe.

Maybe you decide to create a ceremony to accompany this momentous occasion. Buy your favorite food, maybe even a get a cake with candles. You can invite friends to witness and share your cake. Who knows, maybe your friends will want to join you in finding happy! The most important thing about this moment is making it special for you. This is the day you decide to change yourself.

*"Be faithful in small things because it is in them that your strength lies."*

—Mother Teresa

---

## Contract For Happiness

I, _____, hereby commit to my pursuit of finding—and staying—happy.

I promise to put my needs first.

I will love myself for my strengths as well as my weaknesses. My weaknesses are a part of who I am.

I am strong and proud and capable of change.

And I deserve to be happy.

Signed,

Date:

---

## Concrete Action

# Five things that make you happy

What are five things that make you happy? Write them down in your notebook. Got more than five? Great. Keep going! Jot everything that lifts your mood and makes you feel good. This is what you can turn to when you need a literal lift. And it's an important part of finding your happiness.

Make a commitment that you will turn to this list of things that make you happy as often as you need to. These are soul supplements—emotional vitamins. Take as needed!

---

**Selene's Story**

My number one go-to is *The Howard Stern Show*. I've been listening since I was a teenager, when I stumbled upon the show at a time when I was feeling like no one was honest. Howard tells it as he sees it. Plus, he and his team make me laugh! So, Howard Stern is at the top of my list. But I also take other actions when I want to feel happy, like calling my sons or certain friends. What appeals to you?

## Concrete Action

# Acknowledge gratitude

*"Gratitude is the fairest blossom which springs from the soul."*

—Henry Ward Beecher

The saying "count your blessings" is popular for a reason—it's a key element to finding happy.

Break out that notebook and make a list of everything you're grateful for. Better yet, take it a step further to create a gratitude journal by recording the things you're grateful for each day.

Be careful, be choosy, and be honest with yourself about what you are actually grateful for in that moment. Otherwise, it's just words on a piece of paper. Don't just list it—*feel it!*

Another way to practice gratitude is to frame your special pictures and scrapbook your memories. My house is filled with pictures of my sons growing up and beloved notes and cards from them—those boys are certainly my biggest achievement! A glance at any of these mementos sends me into instant gratitude!

I also advise you to frame your own achievements, however big or small.

This is actually one of those times when the smaller things are more important. The smaller things may be more likely to trigger feelings of accomplishment and gratitude over time.

Think about it this way: Diplomas are grand gestures, expensively-framed pieces of paper you proudly hang in a home or business. Diplomas are a physical representation of an achievement that you have gained in exchange for large amounts of your time and money. This sense of accomplishment starts as a direct source of your happiness. It feels amazing, right?But, over time, your brain acclimates to the achievement, and any happiness experienced from a graduation or diploma is *indirect.* Any happiness, or pride, you experience is the result of other people's feelings or reaction. You feel happy because of how *other* people feel about your accomplishment.

This is another reason why it's important to maintain a feeling of constant, in the moment, gratitude.

In case you were curious, science is solidly behind the practice of gratitude as a happiness booster. When you practice gratitude, you're generating serotonin. This is because when you reflect on your past victories and achievements, your brain reacts as though they are happening now, causing you to feel significant. This feeling of importance triggers serotonin production!

## Concrete Action

# Set boundaries

It's important to create boundaries with what you take in from the world. Limit your social media. It's overwhelming and often false—designed to manipulate.

Try to cap how much time you spend reading and answering emails. If your job requires you to do this a lot, try deep breathing while you're reading and responding. Throw away junk mail, remove yourself from newsletters and product mailing lists you don't need.

Cut your interactions with people who drain you. Recognize that no matter how much someone may need your help, you also need to help yourself.

Don't let salespeople suck away your moments with their pitches. My Aunt Olga, a keen observer, called people who take your time, energy, and money "gimmes"—out to grab whatever they can at your expense.

*"An ounce of gold cannot buy an ounce of time."*

—Fortune cookie wisdom

Your time is your most precious commodity, which can never be recovered once spent. Use it well.

If you feel challenged or anxious thinking about boundaries, not to worry! More on establishing them later. I found them quite difficult, too!

## A NOTE FROM THE EXPERT: BRIAN REINTHALER

What if I told you that you could add hours to your day or week?

Everywhere I go, I encounter folks who feel that they never have enough time for the things they *really* want to do. One example was a guy in a small group coaching seminar, and the coach said something that fundamentally changed the way I think about being "too busy."

"This sensation occurs," she said, "when we make the mistake of treating time as a fixed commodity."

I know what you're thinking. Time *is* a fixed commodity! Are there not still sixty minutes in an hour? Twenty-four hours in a day?

Sure, but time is not necessarily a "use it or lose it" proposition.

"We have to remember that our *experience* of time is not that it's fixed at all," the coach said. "Our experience of time is that it's fluid. Time shrinks and expands depending on what we're doing."

Your children may experience this expanding effect the night before Christmas or on a road trip, somewhere between the twelfth and forty-seventh "Are we there yet?" You may experience it in the middle of a tedious day of work or when waiting for test results. When we live not for the present, but for the future, it tends to seem that time slows down.

If you're lucky, you've also experienced the opposite—time flying, we call it. You may be familiar with the sense that an entire day has passed in what seemed like minutes because you were so engrossed in a passion project or a carefree outing with friends.

"The trick to creating the experience of having more time," the coach told the group, "is to do less."

Just as minimizing possessions can reduce physical clutter and create an environment more conducive to creative work and worry-free play, nipping our "busy schedules" in the bud may too bend the space-time continuum in our favor.

Show up ten minutes early to your meetings, meditate for just a few minutes each day (no matter what else you have going on), exercise during your lunch break, or prioritize your hours away from the office as zealously as you do those in it.

*Make Two Lists*

The story goes that one day, legendary investor and one of the wealthiest men in the world, Warren Buffett, approached his long-time pilot, Mike Flint.

He asked Mike about his goals and dreams and suggested that he start by listing his top twenty-five goals, so Mike thought long and hard and eventually returned to Buffett with the prescribed list.

Buffett directed Mike to circle the top five, "the ones you want more than anything."

This was difficult for Mike. Most of his goals were important to him, but he thought he knew where the man—known as the Oracle of Omaha for his sage wisdom—was going with this.

Mike circled his top five, and Buffett made sure they were truly his highest priority. And the rest of the list? Mike said he'd work on those other twenty items as he could. This was where Buffett disagreed with him.

"No," Buffett told him. "You've got it wrong, Mike. Everything you didn't circle just became your 'avoid at all costs' list. No matter what, these things get no attention from you until you've succeeded with your top five."

What Warren Buffet was saying is what I like to think of as *The Power of No.*

Enthusiasm and a can-do attitude are, no doubt, wonderful assets, but when we say "yes" to every assignment, request, and invitation, we invite distraction and mental clutter.

Eliminating the things that distract from your primary goals involves more than simply cutting out obvious wastes of time. It means eliminating work that feels pretty damn important. It means letting go of certain items that you have viewed, until now, as obligations. It means sometimes saying "no" when you're seriously tempted to say "yes."

"No" creates the space in which ambitious and fulfilling goals are achieved.

*Make that Mountain a Molehill*

Personally, I find that lifelong or career goals are a rough place to start. Extended timelines tend to weaken my resolve, so I find more motivational value in short-term goals.

Here is a version of Buffett's advice for Mike that I adapted for myself: Before I start my day, I take a clean piece of paper and write down three to five tasks that are important or causing me stress. They may include things that have been put off from a prior day's list or something that, in that moment, seems urgent.

For each task, I ask myself two questions: "If this is the only thing I accomplish today, will I be satisfied with my day?" and "Will making progress on this task 'sharpen my saw?'" (As in, will it make the other to-do's less important or easier to accomplish later.)

I then remove the items for which I answered "no" to both questions.

From whatever is left, I pick one (and only one), and set aside my next two to three unscheduled hours to focus entirely on this task.

If I have what seems like a million things to accomplish on a given day, I can guarantee I'll accomplish nothing of real value. But when I fully embrace that I cannot do everything, and make the sometimes severe-feeling executive decision to ignore otherwise important tasks, my chance of success on the most important thing soars.

*Brian Reinthaler is a career transition and life coach who believes in challenging his clients to separate what they actually want from what they're "supposed to want" by empowering them to take charge of their lives and move confidently toward where they want to be. A graduate of The University of Notre Dame and Georgetown Law, Brian practiced corporate law in New York for four years and then spent seven years assisting lawyers seeking new jobs as a headhunter, before launching Against the Grain Coaching in 2014. Brian has recently served as a consultant to AltaClaro, heading up the development of continuing education and "soft" skills training programs for attorneys and compliance professionals. You can learn more about Brian at facebook.com/ATGCoach or email him at brian@atgcoach.com*

Concrete Action

# Listen to music

Listening to music can change your mood—and possibly your life. And contrary to what you would expect, any kind of music will due.

Listening to positive, upbeat tunes can lift your mood, especially if you want to feel better.

And what about the sad music we all like to drown ourselves in during breakups or times of family strife? Some evidence suggests that listening to sad music may provide comfort, much like a conversation with a close friend.

Music can also help relieve pain, improve physical health, and result in greater relationship satisfaction.

*"When I hear music, I fear no danger.*
*I am invulnerable. I see no foe.*
*I am related to the earliest times, and to the latest."*

—Henry David Thoreau

Choose songs you love, and if it's possible, have them on a playlist for whenever you need a boost. Try to find ones you somehow relate to (even if you don't know exactly why). But if you have a favorite song that's just loud and fun—go for it! No judgments—especially on yourself.

*"Without music, life is a journey through a desert."*

—Pat Conroy

Maybe you want to create your own music? Take lessons? Pick up where you left off, or learn an instrument you've never tried before?

## Concrete Action

# Sing

*"Singing provides a true sense of lightheartedness. If I sing when I am alone, I feel wonderful. It's freedom."*

—Andrea Bocelli

Spice up your musical choices by singing along—in the car, or at home while you're cooking or cleaning.

Have you ever tried karaoke? Dr. Weisner and I love it.

You can break into song anywhere, as long as you don't get fired for doing it.

### A NOTE FROM THE EXPERT: CANDICE HOYES

The road to music for me began at age two. According to family lore, I would memorize commercial jingles and perform them for all takers, close family members and traveling salespersons alike. Today, many would say I pursue happiness for a living, because I'm a professional musician, specifically a multi-genre vocalist and composer.

I look at my pursuit, which easily gratifies me and expands my imagination, as something that marks my time and connects me across borders and space. Rather than music as a vehicle for happiness, I view my passion as a function of appetite. I express my appetite for life through musical exploration, recording, and performance.

I opt for pursuing my appetite rather than happiness, which seems ever elusive, and lives too close to comfort for my taste. Like appetite, I not only enjoy music, but I also need to consume it. I expect to have it day and night, and this encompasses the necessary sacrifices, discipline, adventure, and often times pleasure that goes with it. That said, my music has the power to bring happiness to a room—and to a listener who feels lonely but for her playlist. It has brought me countless joy-filled moments.

For those folks who want to take up music in any capacity, I offer this good word: Musical happiness is very sweet and to be appreciated. Yet I recommend that one remains loyal to musical pursuit when it brings more challenge than plain happiness. The journey can nonetheless be truly nourishing.

*Candice Hoyes began formal vocal study as an undergraduate at Harvard University, and she was soon gracing the international stages of Carnegie Hall and Lincoln Center as an award-winning classical soloist. In 2015, she toured and recorded with the Jazz at Lincoln Center Orchestra under artistic director Wynton Marsalis, before releasing her own critically-acclaimed album debut,* On A Turquoise Cloud. *Hoyes is the 2019 recipient of both New York City's Arts Engagement and Creative Engagement grants. Hoyes has performed with Lin-Manuel Miranda, Philip Glass, Deepak Chopra, Ira Glass, and Wycliffe Gordon. She will release her second album in 2019. Follow Candice on Instagram @CandiceInColor and on Twitter @CandiceHoyes*

### Selene's Story

 I always loved to sing and majored in chorus at summer camp. (Yes, we had a major and a minor at this camp for the arts—so serious!) Unfortunately, I had a low voice and could not sing any of the female songs. We were doing a production of The Wizard of Oz, and I didn't even bother to audition for Dorothy like most of the girls. Forget about the high notes at the end—I couldn't even reach the opening ones! So I auditioned for the Cowardly Lion. But I didn't get that either. I was cast as an Emerald City resident—about the smallest role (Munchkins were technically smaller—literally, ha ha—but they had more to do on stage). But I sung my heart out.

When I had my kids, my in-home singing career launched. Finally, an enraptured audience! I used to sing "I Want to Be Happy" from the Broadway musical No, No, Nanette to my kids, and my little guy Casey and I sang the theme song to the TV show The Jeffersons together, alternating lines.

My sons are grown now. I sing for my cats.

## Concrete Action

# Meditate

*"Quiet the mind, and the soul will speak."*

—Ma Jaya Sati Bhagavati

Clearing your mind gives it the chance to rest and renew. Doing "nothing" yields amazing results! Find your mantra, and block out those negative thoughts. Meditation and mindfulness are the keys to helping to clear your mind.

Lucky you: You live in an age where you can download a meditation app! Several of them, actually. Don't be afraid to try a few apps until you find one that works for you.

You can also take meditation classes, either online or in person. Transcendental Meditation is awesome to learn, but it is expensive. However, once you learn it you can always come back for free refresher classes.

*"Do what you can, with what you have, where you are."*

—Theodore Roosevelt

Meditation can help you see the possibilities of now.

# A NOTE FROM THE EXPERT: SARAH TEMECH

Although mindfulness is based on ancient Buddhist and Tibetan practices, it has recently come into focus as an easy, accessible way to improve focus and learn effective techniques for relaxation. .

### What exactly is Mindfulness?

Mindfulness is a special way of paying attention to our own experience. As Kabat-Zinn says: On purpose, in the present moment, and without judgment.

Let's take a closer look at that phrase:

*On purpose* means that we intentionally keep our attention on something specific. This could include bodily sensations, sounds occurring around you, or observation of your mental process.

*In the present moment* is a focus on what is happening in the here and now. This means a break from reviewing your to-do list, rehearsing tomorrow's meeting, or ruminating about last week's conversation with your mother. It's paying attention to what's happening right now. And now. And also now.

*Without judgment.* How's that for a challenge? We are often quick to determine good or bad, right or wrong. Act as an observer to your own experience. You aren't there to decide what should or shouldn't be, but simply to notice what is happening, around you or internally.

### So how does focusing on the present make me happier?

A recent research study looked at areas of the brain associated with so-called "mind wandering," which can actually take up fifty percent of our wakeful time. They refer to this area as the default mode network (DMN) and consider it responsible for our "psychological baseline." In other words, where your mind tends to hang out when your attention isn't directed at a specific task. And it turns out, the more time our mind spends wandering, the more unhappy we become.

With all we juggle today, when our mind wanders, it tends to focus on things we are stressed about. The human brain has a stunning ability to plan for the future, process the past, and make creative connections. But when we lose connection with our moment-to-moment experience, we find ourselves spending too much time reliving the past or imagining a meaningful situation.

Researchers speculate that a practice in mindfulness increases bodily and emotional awareness, improving the ability to evaluate and respond to a situation. Imaging studies show that connections between areas of the brain strengthen with the ongoing practice of mindfulness. You are literally training your brain to be happier.

### *How else will this help?*

Sometimes, we rely on autopilot to get through parts of our day. As we squeeze in breakfast, drive to work, or take a shower, our mind is busy in other places. Even our friends and family time is overrun with quick glances at email or down the rabbit hole of social media.

Don't get me wrong, slipping into autopilot has its benefits—as we wash dishes or drive to work, we can mentally multitask to process our past or plan for our future.

But what happens when we get used to running on autopilot? We may become so accustomed to expecting a certain result that we forget to stay in the moment. We forget to listen and observe and we are unable to react to the situation at hand, because we are already (subconsciously) reacting to a situation similar to this that happened in the past. Your boss asks to speak with your after the morning meeting and your stomach tenses up with anticipation. You walk in to see your partner's socks on the floor again and your chest tightens, maybe you snap. Often times, ingrained responses that once served a purpose (as a child a tantrum may have gotten you what you wanted) now serve to confuse or exacerbate a situation. (Imagine how the world would react now if you threw a tantrum every time things didn't go your way.)

Mindfulness acts as a tool to regain control of how you respond to your environment. Mindfulness shows us that between an event occurring and our response is a space. A space that gives you power to choose how you want to react. As we practice mindfulness, we develop our ability to slow down and better tune into ourselves and our environment. This, in turn, allows us to be thoughtful in our reaction. As our interactions become more effective and satisfying, our self-love and self-worth grows. These are qualities directly linked with happiness.

### Still not convinced?

How we talk to ourselves affects our mood. It seems mindfulness works as a way of deepening the relationship with oneself. Psychiatrist Dan Siegel found neurological differences in the social and relationship centers of the brain in participants who practiced mindful meditation. It would make sense that as a relationship with yourself grows, you treat yourself with more kindness, compassion, and acceptance, as you would a dear friend. Isn't that nice?

### Okay, I'm convinced. Do I need to devote my life to meditation now?

Guess what, you can gain these benefits even one minute at a time.

Instructors often start with a focus on the breath. It's constantly flowing and always with you. Try mindful meditation by paying attention to what is happening as the tide of your breath is washing in and out. Note: If a focus on the breath seems to cause anxiety, try a focus on a part of your body that feels safe.

So let's do it now. Set a timer for one minute and close your eyes (if you feel comfortable doing so—another option is a soft downward gaze). Now "observe" your breath for this minute. Bring your attention to a specific area—your chest or stomach rising and falling, the air rushing through your nostrils, or your shoulders moving with each breath. You can even place a gentle hand on that spot to help stay focused. Simply take in that experience in its totality. What is happening to this spot as you take in and release air? How does it move? How is every breath unique in its feel?

Spoiler alert: It is likely that you will start this exercise and think, *Am*

*I doing it?* Or perhaps, *Am I doing it right?* Delete that thought. There is no wrong way to be mindful as long as you maintain the main principles of staying in the present moment and refraining from judgment.

Stop it. Stop judging yourself. This. Is. It. This is mindful meditation.

Another spoiler: Your mind will drift. It's what the mind does. This is not a mindfulness fail, it's part of the process. Mindfulness is a practice in sustained attention, and we only increase our ability to sustain attention with practice, like any other skill. When you've noticed that your mind has drifted, take note and then bring your attention back to your anchor (your focus point).

With practice, you will flow through this process with more ease. And yes, this will increase focus in other areas of your life. For example, schools that incorporated mindfulness into their day reported better performance and decreased inattention among students. Perhaps some incentive to practice with your kids!

### *Grow your practice.*

Work on not getting pulled into your drifting thoughts. It might be important, but save it for later. This is called non-attachment and is another principle of mindfulness. If you find yourself consistently pulled into worry, set aside "worry time." This way your concerns get real attention and you can give yourself permission to take a break from thinking about it at other points in your day.

Remember that thoughts aren't facts. You don't need to react to them as if they are. Repeat this to yourself constantly. Write it on a sticky note and put it on your bathroom mirror. Whatever you gotta do.

Incorporate a practice of mindfulness around gratitude and heartfulness toward others. You are literally changing the pathways of your brain to see more positive in the world.

Looking for guided meditation? Check out these apps: Insight Timer; HeadSpace.

Finally, this poem by Portia Nelson helps me remember that achieving anything takes time and repeated effort. There is no need to be hard on yourself; be encouraging and forgiving.

## *"Autobiography in Five Chapters"*

### *I*

*I walk down the street.*
*There is a deep hole in the sidewalk.*
*I fall in.*
*I am lost…*
*I am hopeless.*
*It isn't my fault.*
*It takes forever to find a way out.*

### *II*

*I walk down the same street.*
*There is a deep hole in the sidewalk.*
*I pretend I don't see it.*
*I fall in again.*
*I can't believe I'm in the same place.*
*But it isn't my fault.*
*It still takes a long time to get out.*

### *III*

*I walk down the same street.*
*There is a deep hole in the sidewalk.*
*I see it is there.*
*I still fall in…it's a habit.*
*My eyes are open; I know where I am;*
*It is my fault.*
*I get out immediately.*

## IV

*I walk down the same street.*
*There is a deep hole in the sidewalk.*
*I walk around it.*

## V

*I walk down another street.*

*Sarah Temech is a mental health counselor working in Brooklyn, NY. She works with children and adults and specializes in depression, anxiety, parenting, interpersonal relationships, and healing from trauma. Sarah is trained in Trauma-Focused Cognitive Behavioral Therapy and Parenting Journey. She uses mindfulness in her personal life and as a tool with clients in counseling. Her interest in mindfulness led Sarah to earn her certificate as a mindfulness educator. Sarah lives in Brooklyn with her husband, three kids, and two dogs, all of whom benefit greatly from her practice in mindfulness. Sarahtemech@yahoo.com*

Concrete Action

# Exercise

Sports and exercise really can make you feel happier, no matter what your age. Adolescents and adults report fewer symptoms of depression when physically active. It turns out all those hours we spend binge-watching sappy television shows and listening to music don't make us as happy as physical activity. In postmenopausal women, a regular cardio and weight routine not only helps combat osteoporosis and other physical ailments, it also works to temper the effects of hormonal changes.

Exercise stimulates your mind and boosts your endorphins. Even the simple act of taking a walk in the fresh air will elevate your spirits. And exercising in a group can boost your endorphins even more!

Maybe you have some friends you can walk, jog, or ride a bike with. If not, how about taking a class at the local gym?

---

## A NOTE FROM THE EXPERT: MATTHEW WALTERS *

I've always been someone who needs to understand "why?"

Why do planes not fall out of the sky? I spent most of my senior year in high school fixating: Exactly how much thrust is required to maintain stable flight for a 747?

I was a sophomore in college when I was first diagnosed with bipolar disorder. That year, one of the most frequently played songs in the dorm was "Lithium," by Nirvana.

Of course, I *needed* to know… why name a song after a lesser-known element in the periodic table?

In 1993, lithium was emerging as the most effective mood stabilizer for a somewhat obscure illness, manic depressive disorder. And the song's writer and lead singer, Kurt Cobain, was the first person I'd ever heard of who had it. That would change quickly.

Within a few months, I wouldn't leave my dorm room. I just couldn't stop crying. When I listened to The Beatles, Paul and John seemed to be telling me to either move to a commune in Vermont or just kill myself and be done with it. I would fall asleep with a ghost of the Virgin Mary glaring judgmentally at me from across the room.

I visited the beach with my best friend late one night. For no reason, I put my hands around his throat and informed him that I could easily kill him before swimming out to sea and never returning. Fortunately, I attempted neither.

That night, I cried myself to sleep on the kitchen floor, lacking the energy to climb the stairs to bed. Thankfully, my roommate had informed my parents of the situation and they came to remove me from school the next day. When they found me on the bottom of the stairs the next morning, I immediately told them that I wanted to be hospitalized. Unbeknownst to me, they were already researching local mental hospitals.

I was treated in a locked unit on suicide watch for five weeks and diagnosed with manic depression. It took months, or maybe years, for me to fully come to terms with this label, but at the time, there was great relief in simply having an answer.

Suddenly, there was an explanation for the occasional "highs" I experienced between periods of normalcy or prolonged depression. My highs weren't the good times. They weren't sex, drugs, and rock 'n' roll the way mania is portrayed in the movies. It just wasn't my style.

Instead, I would fixate on something—maybe a research topic like Greek philosophy or an otherwise boring work project—and work furiously on it without sleep. It felt like everyone around me was operating in slow motion, and I was just getting a lot done.

Inevitably, this would result in a crash of depression.

Today, this disease is known as bipolar disorder. And this "cycling" of emotions, of highs and lows, is why this disease takes longer to identify and properly diagnose. This cycling is also why it is so difficult to find the right medication to effectively treat the disease.

But to my young, overly-analytical brain, a diagnosis of manic depression didn't mean that it was a disease that would take some time to properly medicate.

Eventually, I bounced back from my college experience and returned to a semi-normal existence. Or, as normal an existence as possible, since it seemed pretty clear that this diagnosis of manic depression meant that I was absolutely insane. Or, at least, that's what the books and notes and research that I hungrily devoured each day in the hospital seemed to say. At the very least, it was made quite clear to me that from this point on, I would spend the rest of my life checking in and out of hospitals.

I would not be able to have a job or a wife or a family. I would not be able to continue my quest in finding answers to the many *why* questions that had pressed me my entire life.

Four years after the initial onslaught of mental illness, it was clear that none of the available mood stabilizers (including lithium) were an effective treatment for me. Eventually, my psychiatrist suggested ECT (electro-convulsive therapy).

I wasn't as surprised as you might think. I had done plenty of research on alternative treatments—maybe even more than I did on that whole 747 thrust question. And, yes, I was truly terrified that my doctor and I were discussing, and contemplating, this so-called barbaric procedure that I associated solely with Mary Shelley's *Frankenstein*.

But I was also truly terrified at the thought that I might never find a way to treat my disease. I just wanted to be able to get back to work and be productive.

Six weeks and eight ECT treatments later, my symptoms disappeared. But I quickly discovered that, along with my depression and mania, I had also lost the memory and understanding of the programming language I used each day at work.

I was better in so many ways, but felt lost in so many others. To this day, there are gaps in my memory about people and places and conversations that occurred for up to a year after my treatment. I was working, I was functioning, and I was certain that the only people I saw or heard were real. But I still wasn't me.

As I was pedaling through the fog of my mind, a new, fitness-minded friend encouraged me to quit smoking and run with her. I wish I could remember what she said, because when I tell the story now, it seems more like a poignant moment in a movie than a powerful memory of my recovery. I wish I could tell you why and how I walked away from the cigarettes that had been my lifeline throughout my illness, and why the idea of running a bunch seemed like a good way to spend my time.

But I can't. I just remember running.

After running a few 5k and 10k races, I turned my attention to my favorite sport as a kid: cycling. Several months later, I attempted my first triathlon.

By the time I reached the finish line, I knew I was hooked. Within two years, I had finished a triathlon that included a 1.5-mile swim from Alcatraz Island to the shores of San Francisco and a half-Iron distance (56-mile bike ride, and a 13.1-mile run) race in Florida two weeks later.

To be clear: I am mediocre at best even now, many years later. I don't compete to place or to beat a fellow competitor. Instead, I compete against myself to get faster, stronger, or finish more difficult events. That's it. My many medals are for finishing, not winning. And I'm totally okay with that.

Through these triathlons, I finally found my inner strength and my outside support system. These people became my community. Most of my triathlete friends weren't aware of my illness, but they were my allies nonetheless. And I am theirs.

To this day, I hold true to the belief that if you wake up at 5am for a quick swim before work and fit a 5k run in at lunch all so you can *finish*—not win—a race, you're both a winner and my ally. Whatever the reason, they're trying to better themselves just as I am, and are therefore an inspiration to me.

As I've come to learn, many triathletes have demons we battle with our daily sweat sessions. No matter what those demons are, we all seem to feel better when we physically fight our way through to the finish line. First place or last, we finish and remain at the finish line to see and celebrate the last person to come through. Sometimes, the last person is a 92-year-old man who just keeps pushing on at any pace. He deserves the respect of our cheers as he crosses the finish line.

I am continually amazed and inspired by blind athletes outpacing me on the run (they run with guides to verbally direct them), and by para-tri-athletes competing with just one arm or no legs. I have seen significantly overweight beginners lose a hundred pounds over the course of their first season. I once met an eighty-something-year-old nun who was the oldest woman to have finished an Ironman.

Triathlons are about continually re-inventing yourself by pushing past what you thought were your limits. We feed off the energy of a supportive community and then repeat the process in the next race, or the next season.

And this is exactly what I have done with my illness for the last twenty years. I have a job that I take pleasure in, since it provides me with ample opportunity to answer the *why* questions in the world. I have important relationships with others, and I have a tremendously supportive family to get me through the rough times, since by now I understand that there will always be a better time ahead.

Many of my friends can't wait to work out. Not me! Most days I need to force myself, but I know I'll feel better afterwards. That daily struggle is my constant recognition of—and fight against—the demons inside me and the depression they can cause.

And for nearly twenty years now, my doctors have considered me in remission.

I never did finish college, but I've founded three successful companies and am now an IT consultant. I answer a lot of *whys*. Oh, and along the way I founded a local triathlon club and was elected to triathlon's governing body, USA Triathlon.

Is it the sweat and endorphins? The past ECT treatments? Daily anti-depressants? Maybe it's all of the above—I have to accept that I can never know the complete "why." But I do know that I'll continue my daily battle through exercise for as long as I can; hopefully at least to age 92 like that young-at-heart guy I mentioned above. It's my support system, my medication, my therapy, and my group therapy all in one.

Sadly, as my battle with bipolar was beginning, singer Kurt Cobain's ended with his suicide. Since that day, I've always sworn to myself I would do whatever it took to not share that fate.

And to anyone reading this who is struggling, my advice is to go for a long walk or get on a bike. It's not a cure, but it may serve as enough of a distraction that you can hold on for one more day.

My sport may not be for you, but there are plenty of other sports out there. Give it a try. Find a supportive community and sweat with them like your life depends on it.

*Matthew Walters\* is in bipolar remission. He is an entrepreneur and a tech guru whose creative mind has helped to solve many* why *questions for organizations throughout the country. Thus far, he has not consulted on the thrust of a 747, nor has he managed to convince Scarlett Johansson and Jennifer Lawrence to simultaneously give him their hand(s) in marriage. But one day he might.*
*\*Not his real name*

Concrete Action

# Dance

*"Dance is the hidden language of the soul."*

—Martha Graham

Work it!

Science teaches us that movement gets those endorphins going—brain chemicals/hormones/neurotransmitters (take your pick on how you'd like to refer to them)—which promote jubilation and gratification, as well as high pain tolerance. You can't help but feel better. But there's something extra mood-uplifting about dance. So much so, that some people take "dance therapy" to feel better psychologically.

Perhaps it's the addition of music to the equation. Maybe it's the patterns, which humans find comforting. Could be the satisfaction of learning steps and routines. (This last one definitely doesn't apply to me. I have zero coordination. But I dance anyway. I'm just not trying to win any contests.) Maybe it's the internal rhythm that gets flowing.

Whatever it is, it works!

## A NOTE FROM THE EXPERT: DOMINIQUE ANDRIESE

I needed to make a serious decision. My acting career was at a standstill. I was stuck. Stagnant. I needed a life saver, but I didn't know where to look. Obviously, the most logical next step was an internet search. Maybe, l would find my calling… or at least another paying gig.

I found a gig. A short-term solution, or so I thought. I would be teaching creative movement to children with autism at the New York Institute for Special Education. Teaching dance wasn't far-fetched for me. I had graduated from Hofstra University as a speech communications and rhetorical studies major with a minor in dance. And it wasn't so long ago that I had resigned from my job as a preschool teacher.

I figured this new dance gig would provide me with money, opportunity to continue exploring my acting career, and time to figure out my next step. Little did I know, I had stumbled onto the building blocks of who I am today: a dance/movement therapist.

I knew I was doing something cool with the autistic children I was working with, but at the time I had no idea that there was a science to what I was doing. I simply created a safe space for these children to move their bodies, listen to music, and not be weighed down by their cognitive, physical, and emotional limitations. I saw them as individuals and treated them with love.

The other teachers were impressed by the work I did and wanted to know if I could teach them. Could I? First, I needed to find out what the h-e-double-hockey-sticks I was doing. It felt like magic, but my Google research told me that it was much more. The work that I had been doing with my students was a form of dance/movement therapy. I was slightly pissed, slightly disappointed, because a part of me had been thinking that

I might have invented a new profession. But more than that, I was blown away that dance/movement therapy was a thing!

I began to put all my energy getting into the Master of Science program at Sarah Lawrence College.

So, what exactly is dance music therapy? It is the use of movement to promote emotional, social, cognitive, and physical integration of the individual, for the purpose of improving health and well-being.

It began in the 1940s, when professional dancers began to realize the benefit of using dance and movement as a form of therapy. It is a holistic approach to healing, based on the belief that the mind and body are related and inseparable. Changes in the body reflect changes in the mind, and vice versa.

Today, I am the first dance/movement therapist for the Elizabeth Seton Pediatric Center. I work with medically fragile children in palliative care. These children have life-limiting illnesses, and I am part of a team of people who focus on providing relief from the symptoms, pain, physical stress, and mental stress at any stage of illness.

These beautiful children suffer from the most complex diagnoses, but through the use of dance/movement therapy I celebrate who they are and highlight their abled self. It is my job to meet these children where they are to begin a conversation and to offer a sense of healing through dance and movement.

Working with my clients has given me much joy. I see these children as abled-functioning little ones, no matter if non-verbal or facing a life-threatening illness. I work to strip away the heaviness of life's pressures some of these children face. I have the knowledge to assess movement, create treatment plans, and implement interventions to reach short or long-term goals.

Dance/movement therapy can look differently for each group member. As long as you pay attention to what feels good to you, you can experience great joy even in the smallest movement, like the subtlety of paying attention to your breath. Here are ten helpful tips you may need as a gentle reminder when life's moments get rough.

1.  Breathe in. Hold it. Keep holding it. Release.

2.  Notice the quality of your breath. Is it deep or shallow? Take note.

3. Now take another breath in. Before you release, I want you to visualize a word that describes the source of your anguish, if any.

4. When you have that word, take a deep breath and release again, seeing the word vanish with the release of your breath.

5. Now breathe in "love" to the part of your body that needs it the most. For example, if your neck needs love, touch your neck as you breathe in and exhale that energy that may be holding you back. There's power in the therapeutic touch. Therapeutic touch, known by some as "non-contact therapeutic touch," is a pseudo-scientific energy therapy that practitioners claim promotes healing and reduces pain and anxiety.

6. Slowly roll your shoulders backwards (repeat five times).

7. Slowly roll your shoulders forward (repeat five times).

8. Take a deep breath.

9. Slowly move your head up, down, left, and right (repeat five times).

10. Slowly roll your head in a circle (repeat five times).

These ten tips can be done on the train, driving in your car, before a major meeting, after a stressful interview, while at a busy grocery store, or even when you have to face a difficult situation. No longer at a crossroad, I took a leap of faith. I can barely pay my bills (joking, slightly), nevertheless I remain thankful that dance/movement therapy found me.

*Dominique Andriese's first acting gig was for MC Lyte, playing a "Younger Lyte" in the music video "Like as a rock." In 2010 she co-starred with Michael Ealy in Our-Time Theater Company's* Three One-Act Plays. *In 2012 Dominique wrote and produced her first Off-Broadway production,* Waiting in Line. *After graduating with a Master's in dance/movement therapy from Sarah Lawrence College, Dominique started her own business, DASITF Therapy. She specializes in working with children with emotional, mental, and physical disabilities. For more information, contact her at DASTIF@gmail.com.*

*"Dance, when you're broken open. Dance, if you've torn the bandage off. Dance in the middle of the fighting. Dance in your blood. Dance when you're perfectly free."*

—Rumi

Notice how children dance. They don't worry about what people think; they're not self-conscious about it at all. They dance in joy.

Yes, dance is most definitely linked to joy.

*"And those who were seen dancing were thought to be insane by those who could not hear the music."*

—Attributed to Friedrich Nietzsche
*(but not absolutely proven he wrote it)*

I believe that we can all hear the music, if we allow ourselves to. It's just that so many of us have been shamed out of dancing. We've shut down, slumped into a stupor, not even conscious of our oblivion. It's time to rise. It's time to dance again.

*"Dance like no one is watching.*
*Sing like no one is listening.*
*Love like you've never been hurt.*
*And live like it's heaven on Earth."*

—Mark Twain

## Concrete Action

# Embrace art

*"Art washes from the soul the dust of everyday life."*

—Pablo Picasso

Art inspires you. My favorite artist is Claude Monet, the French Impressionist. Impressionism, to me, is like a dream you've been invited to share in and from which you form your own impression! It's evocative and inspires my mind to create. They say that every picture tells a story, and Monet's paintings tell me love stories. I feel his love of nature and environment, and the ever-shifting connections between the natural world and human lives.

*"Everyone discusses my art and pretends to understand, as if it were necessary to understand, when it is simply necessary to love."*

—Claude Monet

I discovered Monet on a school trip to France when I was in eighth grade. I love how Monet painted the same scene in different lighting and shades. Each painting in a series tells its own story, even though it's the same setting as the others. His most famous paintings are of his water lily pond and the bridge over it. I visited his home with my sons. It was a joy sharing this artist with my sons and seeing their perspective. Consider sharing art with your family and friends!

What moves you?

Who is your favorite artist?

What is it about them that draws you in?

If you don't have one yet, why not start looking?

## A NOTE FROM THE EXPERT: MEREDITH SAMUELSON

Necessity is the mother of invention, and I am the mother of two young boys who refuse to wear store-bought Halloween costumes. Over piles of cardboard scraps, shreds of felt, and sticky plaster gauze, obscure video game characters rise from the ashes. I am met with the immediate gratification of happy exclamations and soft hugs when these costumes come to fruition, but there is another fulfillment involved. There is a deep satisfaction that comes from the problem solving of crafting.

Building, writing, painting, and countless other creative activities employ our problem-solving skills. But even sitting down with a Lego kit and a set of instructions can satisfy the need to create. It is the process that is crucial to happiness, because, as psychologist Frank Barron wrote, "when we make, repair, or create things we feel vital and effective." Barron was considered a pioneer in studying the psychology of creativity. In further research on the topic, psychologist Kelly Lambert explored the link between hand-use and mood and found that, "hands-on work satisfies our primal need to make things."

For me, there aren't many things that give me a greater kick than saying yes to a project I have no idea how I'll manifest. From drawing on past experience and imagination, I know I have the skills to figure it out and the confidence to agree to the task. And beyond the feelings of pride and determination, I may even be healthier for it.

According to the paper "Happiness and Longevity in the United States" that appeared in the journal *Social Science & Medicine*, "Happy people typically enjoy better health outcomes because they demonstrate more successful adaptation; better problem-solving skills and coping strategies; more creative, imaginative, and integrative thinking; greater resilience; and a greater ability to deal with adversity."

So how can you get started?

Go back to all of those Pinterest pins you've saved, or visit your nearest crafts store where you're likely to find seasonal inspiration. Pick a project with manageable materials. (If you've never crafted before, it will probably be overwhelming to commit to custom hand-painted wedding centerpieces.)

I love projects with materials you probably already have on hand, like painting rocks from your garden or using leftover paint swatches to create a pretty garland. If you're lacking inspiration, look for projects that are functional and meaningful. Make a handmade card for a friend. Create a one-of-a-kind tote bag with a cheap canvas bag and a printable iron-on. Think about some of the skills you already have and repurpose them. Can you sew a little bit? Try creating a simple and silly sock doll. The more you do, the more you'll realize you're able to do.

You might be surprised to discover how quickly and wholly you've found yourself totally immersed in a project. Experts call that immersion "flow," and it's actually great for your wellbeing. The psychologist Mihaly Csikszentmihalyi defined "flow" as being "in the zone," as in being lost in the activity and not marking the passing of time. A good life, he has argued, is one in which this state is not so elusive. While flow can come from all kinds of activities, art is one of the classic flow experiences, where the art-maker is fully engaged in the process.

Once you've found a craft you enjoy, abandon your notions of perfection. It doesn't exist, and it isn't important. The little blemishes and missteps make your projects uniquely yours. Entire art forms have embraced the concept of purposeful flaws and blatant brushstrokes. It reminds us that your hands and your hard work guided your vision.

And if you, like I, have little ones climbing into a homemade cardboard spaceship, they're hardly likely to notice the crooked rocket boosters when they're suiting up and blasting off.

*Meredith Samuelson is an artist and middle school art teacher in Brooklyn, New York. Her artwork has been featured in* Time Out New York *and her writing in the parenting anthology,* So Glad They Told Me: Women Get Real About Motherhood. *She finds her flow in customizing sneakers, bags, and other random surfaces and in being a certified #momofboys. Contact her at meris111@hotmail.com*

# A NOTE FROM THE EXPERT: NICOLE LEE

The recent push to market coloring books toward adults is more than just a clever fad. The simple act of coloring can be used as a way to find stress relief, relaxation, and restore a feeling of calm in the hectic world that too quickly pulls us out of balance.

Art therapy is a combination of theory, creative expression, process, and the therapeutic relationship. Through nonverbal and verbal communication, the client is able to explore emotions and feelings in order to obtain personal growth. When we are able to feel empowered through the use of creative arts, positive change can occur just as an art piece transforms from beginning to end.

Stress affects chemical triggers, including blood pressure, heart rate, and mental focus, which are all very much interconnected in the functioning of the human body. The nervous, hormonal, and immune systems are immediately affected by stressful events. Exposure to prolonged stress makes people more susceptible to physical and emotional illnesses. Therefore, utilizing the arts as a tool for stress reduction may prove to be beneficial to improving how one copes with stress and its effect on the mind and body.

Why art for stress reduction? Line, form, and color are components of the symbolic language of art. In addition to these basic principles, the elements of texture, depth, volume, space, movement, and abstraction are also communicated representations recognized within artwork. These elements provide an expression of one's character through a visual language. Art can expose and provoke feelings that are undeniable to the human soul and the human psyche. The mind and the body react in ways that indicate emotions and thought patterns are prevalent in the art making process.

Through the use of coloring books, adults are seemingly willing to explore alternative approaches as a way to rest and restore. This pre-verbal activity of making art and coloring continues to prove, through lines, shapes, textures, and colors, that the creative arts are easily accessible and readily available to all ages.

With the guidance and support of a licensed art therapist, individuals are able to creatively self-express, which is recognized as a pertinent aspect to the therapeutic process. This can help develop a stronger sense of self, process overwhelming thoughts or feelings, and implement positive coping skills, which are used to help manage challenges or frustrations.

Art making can be utilized independently at home as a way to de-stress and engage in the simple act of being aware of how one works with the art materials. Incorporating art making into your daily activities is a great first step to understanding how this modality may serve you. Below, you can follow a step-by-step guide for finding a sense of ease and promoting a positive self-care routine through art making.

1.  Purchase a personal journal that speaks to you, with blank pages appropriate for doodling. This journal can be large, small, or somewhere in between. Choose a size that feels manageable to work with.

2.  Find art materials that stand out to you at your local craft store, like markers, colored pencils, or oil pastels. They do not have to be a high-end brand; buy materials that are in your price range. On a budget? No problem. Collage art allows you to collect found materials from your own home or even the outdoors to be glued into your journal. Old magazine clippings are also a great source for inspiration and collaging.

3.  Now that you have all of your art materials on hand, pick a day and time you can dedicate at least fifteen to thirty minutes to this journal.

4.  No previous art skills are necessary. There is no right or wrong way to make art! Let go of any expectations you may have set.

5.  Take a deep breath. Before creating art, it may be helpful to take several deep breaths as a way to center yourself. Once you feel you are at place in your body where you feel at ease, continue.

6.  Start with a theme or an intention. For example, today's intention is letting go of perfection. Then go ahead and create art without

the worry of making it look a certain way. On a different day you may choose to stick with the same theme or try something new, like self-love. Your goal is to allow yourself to create an art piece that is meaningful to you when you think of "self-love."

7. Go in with no theme. It can be anything! Begin to pick colors or materials that stand out and create shapes or designs that feel right for you in the moment.

8. Take small breaks when needed. Be gentle with yourself and try to let go of any criticisms that may come up as you make art. Remember, this exercise is not a graded experience. You can choose to keep your work private or share it with others.

9. When finished with the page, take several deep breaths once more and reflect to yourself that this journal is a secure place where all drawings are accepted and appreciated.

10. Congratulations! You have completed your first page! Now it's time to schedule your next session for self-care journaling.

Creative art making may be used as a therapeutic tool to reducing daily stress, however it is important to note that art-making for some may feel best supported under the guidance of a licensed creative arts therapist or mental health professional.

*Nicole Lee is a clinical psychotherapist and yoga instructor. She holds an art therapy license in New York State, LCAT, a board certification as an art therapist, ATR-BC, and a registered yoga instructor, RYT. Nicole has experience working with children and families who have experienced complex trauma. She is trained in EMDR and mindfulness techniques, which are interwoven within her therapeutic approach. Most recently, Nicole opened a private practice located in Long Beach, NY, where she provides creative arts therapy to children, adults, and couples. For more information about her services and workshops, visit www.NicoleLeeTherapy.com*

## Concrete Action

# Read literature

*"Literature adds to reality, it does not simply describe it. It enriches the necessary competencies that daily life requires and provides; and in this respect, it irrigates the deserts that our lives have already become."*

—C.S. Lewis

An interesting quote coming from the creator of The Chronicles of Narnia! But even when we read fantasy, literature clarifies and amplifies reality—because emotions are at its core.

Literature adds to our perceptions. It gives us "aha" moments of clarity and empathy, when we bond with the characters we're following.

And literature is a dose of shared humanity. It's evidence that you're not alone in your struggles. As the novelist Stephen Wright, my writing teacher, told our class: "Literature says, 'Wake up' to your soul."

*"Literature is one of the most interesting and significant expressions of humanity."*

—P. T. Barnum

Literature will help you realize just what's inside you.

*"Do not feel lonely. The entire universe is inside of you."*

—Rumi

You will never feel lonely while reading a novel.

---

## Concrete Action

# Be dramatic

Watching or participating in a theater group isn't just fun and plays.

Did you know that watching a dramatic scene increases social bonding? Are you surprised to hear that pain tolerance increases after viewing a dramatic performance? And for older adults, viewing live theater increases a feeling of belonging, a willingness to engage socially, and positive mood.

There are also benefits for people who are brave enough to step on the stage themselves. High school theater participation appears to pave the way for the potential for workplace success in the future, and thespians of all ages tend to have a greater ability to correctly identify their own emotions and the emotions of others, which can help them to communicate better.

So why not give it a try? Be bold and brave and find a local theater group that holds open auditions. Or if you're not ready to step into the spotlight, offer your services behind the scenes. Theater troupes are always looking for help with costumes, set design, and much more.

---

## A NOTE FROM THE EXPERT: DR. ALISA HURWITZ

As clinical psychologists, we often reach inside of our tool bag to refer patients to reading material to supplement their work in session. Bibliotherapy can be a useful resource, especially for those who enjoy consuming written information. Sometimes the recommendations are general, like prescribing *The Anxiety & Phobia Workbook* to new patients who are presenting with symptoms of anxiety as a supplement to our in-office therapeutic work. Other times, the recommendations are more specific and novelistic, such as suggesting Cheryl Strayed's memoir *Wild* for a patient who is reconnecting with herself through long-range hiking.

Not every patient, however, is an avid reader. In trying to meet them where they are at, I explore what art or popular culture speaks to them, including movies, photography, pop music, comic books, and more.

Since my own cultural language is musical theater, I am most adept at sending my patients to check out a specific song, cast album, or live performance as a way to help them understand their own experiences with mental health, especially for those who are fellow theater "geeks."

At times, I recommend a particular show because the individual is dealing with the same issues as the characters, and the music can offer catharsis or insight. The 2009 Broadway musical *Next to Normal* focuses on an intimate family drama. It's centered around the mother, Diana Goodman, who has bipolar disorder. The song "I Miss the Mountains" perfectly illuminates the common experience of folks with a bipolar mood disorder who choose to stop taking their mood stabilizer psychotropic medication because they miss the highs of the mania.

The current hit *Dear Evan Hansen* is another cast album that I regularly refer to patients. This is a show centered on an anxious teenager who struggles with social interactions and virtually vibrates when talking to his peers. The song "Waving Through a Window" is an insightful piece about the desire to connect but the anxiety that stands in the way. Part of the reason this show is such a hit is the way the songwriters (Justin Paul and Benj Pasek) evoke the interior experience of anxiety. Look at the lyrics to "Waving Through a Window": "I try to speak, but nobody can hear / So I wait around for an answer to appear / While I'm watch, watch, watching people pass / I'm waving through a window." Lyrics like that have resonated with hundreds of thousands of anxiety sufferers.

There are moments when I know that someone sitting across from me in my office needs some pure light and affirmation. Shows like *Kinky Boots*, which enthusiastically encourages us to "just be with dignity," or *Head*

*Over Heels*, which uses the music of the hit all-female band, The Go-Go's, to celebrate uniqueness and truth to self.

Musical theater, when viewed live, also offers the benefits of being in-the-moment and communal. The experience of seeing the musical *Come From Away* is to feel moved by community and kindness, both on the stage and in congregation with the audience. This show is the true story of what happened on Sept. 11, 2001, when thirty-eight airplanes were diverted to the provincial airport in Gander, Newfoundland, and the locals welcomed the passengers with love and open arms. There is no facsimile for the feeling of sitting next to others in the theater, knowing that you only have each other in the face of a crisis, and that kindness truly matters.

Whether it's for catharsis or escapist joy, having a communal experience, or just something that is true, musical theater has something to offer for any and every mood. It's a great tool for self-discovery and trying to understand the human experience. If it is an art form that speaks to you, go, listen, watch, and feel seen.

------

When you think about it, clinicians have been using theater to guide and shape the actions of their patients for years.

Ever heard of role play?

Of course you have. But I bet you don't know where it comes from.

Romanian psychiatrist Jacob Moreno was the first to coin the term "role play," although his earlier concept of the "theatre of spontaneity" referred to a similar idea. Moreno believed that the best way for individuals to conquer the past – in particular their past interpersonal conflicts – was to find a way to redo and/or undo them in the present. And, of course, this revision of sorts would then allow the patient to be better able to handle future conflicts.

Moreno's "psychodrama" technique involved the patient and the therapist recalling – and essentially reliving – a previous conflict, trauma, or otherwise stressful situation in an attempt to better understand the underlying dynamics that the patient may not have been aware of in the moment of the stressor.

Then, the second part of the psychodrama technique, has the patient and the therapist change "roles," so that the patient is able to see the other person's perspective.

This technique has proven to be quite helpful when working with children, families, and couples. In fact, the Gottman Method (a couples therapy-focused modality) relies heavily on this ability to switch perspectives and see what it feels like to be in your partner's shoes, so to speak.

So what does this mean for the multitude of "role-playing" games that have spanned the ages from the classic Dungeons and Dragons to the more recent first-person shooter video games?

The answer should be obvious: it just depends.

As long as the role-playing game allows for the player or players to see both sides of a war/conflict/magical-mystical world, there is the opportunity for learning and growth to occur.

Theater, both participation in and observation of, can provide the same opportunity for personal growth and fostering a more open-minded attitude.

*Dr. Alisa Hurwitz is a clinical psychologist and writer. She practices at The Counseling Center of Nashua in southern New Hampshire, specializing in family therapy, autism spectrum disorders, gender identity, and trauma. She maintains a blog and interview site that focuses on the intersection of theater and psychology. You can read more of her articles and interviews with Broadway actors and creatives at www.drdrama.com.*

# A NOTE FROM THE EXPERT: SANDEE LEONHARD

*"Food, glorious food...."* Alex stood center stage and belted out the tune. His teachers were amazed. His classmates were amazed. His mother was crying.

Everyone in the audience knew that after his father died, Alex had become quiet, shy, and removed. I was one of very few people who knew that soon after his father's death, he developed an eating disorder. I couldn't remember the last time I saw him smile, and yet here he was. It didn't matter that he sang beautifully, and that he nailed every note—although he did both. What amazed everyone was that Alex was standing center stage, singing!

Finding a home on stage gave Alex confidence, happiness, and a place to shine.

Through my work as a drama educator, I have met many Alexes. I have seen children begin a rehearsal process reserved and unsure then blossom through their work in the creative arts. There's something magical about performing. And for me, guiding my young students through the process is just as magical.

While it may be easy to think that being on stage, being in the spotlight, is an "all about me" experience, it is quite the opposite. Theater is about sharing that experience. For some, like Alex, acting might be a way to temporarily escape from the troubles of real life. Theater can be a daydream that they share with other people. It's about connecting on stage in an honest, truthful way, both with your castmates and your audience.

Participating in theater has also been shown to increase empathy in children. After all, to act as someone else, you must put yourself in someone else's shoes. What better way is there to teach empathy to youngsters?

Through children's work in theater, they are learning valuable life skills—life skills that lead to a productive, happier life.

My education in theater taught me perseverance and what a good work ethic is. It taught me about passion and gave me self-confidence. Through my work in theater, I learned what a real deadline is and how to work under pressure. Being involved in my school plays taught me what it means to be a participating community member and to trust and be trusted. For Alex, I hope the lessons of empathy, of sharing the spotlight, and of pride will shape his adult life. They certainly did mine.

*Sandee Leonhard is the happy, proud owner of Drama Kids of South Nassau, a developmental drama program for children. She is passionate about building self-esteem and confidence in young people. Sandee has taken her talents abroad to work in children's theater internationally, including Israel and Greece. Sandee lives in Long Island, New York, where she continues to help children discover the creative outlet of theater. She can be reached at dramakidsnassau@optonline.net.*

## Concrete Action

# Seek out comedy

*"Like a welcome summer rain, humor may suddenly cleanse and cool the earth, the air and you."*

—Langston Hughes

Take your mind to a happy place!

*"Even the gods love jokes."*

—Plato

43

As I mentioned earlier, Howard Stern is my go-to for instant happiness.

> *"I believe I am doing the work for humanity. This show is so uplifting."*
>
> —Howard Stern

I agree that Howard's humor helps humanity, and so would the rest of his millions of fans. Comedy exposes a truth we know and relate to—we laugh because we're in on the joke. The joke is life; the joke is us. Howard brings us together to laugh at the absurdity of us. And to those who say *The Howard Stern Show* is obscene, I say: life is obscene, and the show mirrors life. Sometimes it's a fun house mirror, but sometimes it's an absolutely real image we're presented with. I think people who have a problem looking at their real selves are the people who have a problem with Howard Stern.

If you haven't listened to Howard, I highly recommend doing so. Howard is all I listen to… thanks to the technology we have. I listen in my car, in my house, in my headphones as I take a walk—he lifts my heart instantly. I tell you, you can't be in a bad mood while you're listening to Howard Stern.

No matter what kind of comedy appeals to you, you can find it with ease these days. Dry, subtle, off-the-wall—there's such variety! Take some time to discover what funny entertainment jives with you.

> *"Mirth is God's medicine."*
>
> —Henry Ward Beecher

Comedy will lead to you the next highly recommended action:

## Concrete Action

# Laugh

Laughter heals and raises your spirit!

Scientific studies have shown that laughing (even forced laughter) reduces the level of the "stress hormone" cortisol in the body. It's a distraction from pain and stress. It makes you forget to worry—and if it can make you forget to worry, it might even make you forget to cry. Laughter triggers the release of endorphins.

*"Laughter is an instant vacation."*

—Milton Berle

*"With the fearful strain that is on me night and day, if I did not laugh I should die."*

—Abraham Lincoln

Laughter keeps you focused in the present moment, so you cannot dwell on past sorrows and failures, or fret about what the future will hold.

Try laughing at your worries, or joking about them! After all, this is what comedians do.

*"As soon as you have made a thought, laugh at it."*

—Lao Tsu

*"Always laugh when you can. It is cheap medicine."*

—Lord Byron

*"As soap is to the body, so laughter is to the soul."*

—A Jewish Proverb

Laughter helps you see the world in a different light and shakes things up that may have been stagnant or immobilized inside of us. A door opens—you are free to walk away from your woes.

And to walk toward your new possibilities!

---

## A NOTE FROM THE EXPERT: PETER GROSSMAN

There is a great '80s movie called *Real Genius*, which, among many other things, serves as the answer to the question, "How the hell did Val Kilmer book both *Top Gun*'s Iceman *and Batman*?" He is truly brilliant in the movie, playing Chris Knight, a party animal, super smart kid in a special school full of (non-party animal) super smart kids.

There is a fantastically memorable scene where the super smart kids—in an act of defiance against the evil adults who have made them unknowingly work on a massive laser weapon that only super smart kids could build—point said laser at their popcorn-smell-hating professor's house, setting off a giant Jiffy Pop-like device which fills the house with glorious deliciousness. (This is relevant because the scene is awesome, and I now want popcorn.)

However, there is another scene in the movie in which our heroes are facing seemingly insurmountable odds against the evil adults—a pivotal plot point in every good '80s movie—where Val Kilmer's character turns to the dorky, smart kid sidekick he's trying to mentor and forces said nerd to simply… laugh. Maniacally.

Unsurprisingly, this works in the movie.

Slightly more surprisingly, this works in real life, too. And not just in an '80s movie montage kind of way. It really does! Try it. Go find a place you're comfortable in. Maybe your bathroom or, if you're feeling edgy, a quiet place outside. Now do it. But *really* do it. Laugh maniacally like you've just invented a laser to fill your professor's house full of popcorn. Give it a full MWAHAHA!

I'll wait here.

See? I bet you're smiling now! That's because your body is being flooded with endorphins, the hormones that, to use a technical, scientific term befitting my status in the community, make you feel all warm and fuzzy and stuff. Laughter and happiness aren't connected by a one-way street. It makes sense that when you're happy, the laughter that comes is the result of that happiness, and that is sometimes true. But it's also the case that the act of laughter itself releases endorphins. Not only are we happy when we're laughing, but laughing reduces pain and increases our tolerance to pain. These are the same hormones that are coursing through our bodies when we exercise or have an orgasm. It's powerful stuff!

So, how do you do it? What is it that makes us laugh? There's an old adage that comedy = tragedy + time, but I don't think I agree with that. With all that the mental health community now knows about trauma, it seems to me that comedy is better served by an absence of tragedy.

Also, someone slipping on a banana peel is instantly hilarious—so much for time being necessary! I think for something to be funny, it needs to start by being different than what was expected. The camera shows a tight shot of a man's tearful face confessing his undying love, but when the shot pans back, you can see that he is speaking to his pet turtle. There's nothing inherently funny about love or tears or turtles (actually, that's a lie: sometimes, rarely, always, in that order, but I digress).

Still, it's the unexpected that often makes things humorous.

Imagine an existence where only the expected happened. Would you ever feel anything? Those little jolts we get when something *other* happens—the "goose" after a dozen "ducks"—are where all of our pain and pleasure come from.

The trouble with the unexpected is that fear of the unknown = stress = unhappiness (and yes, that's a proven mathematical equation). That makes unexpected things start from a place of weakness! Funny things are antithetical to our fight or flight survival tendencies. Doesn't that suck? Look, no one said being happy was easy! Finding more space for laughter or having what we call a "sense of humor" requires a certain degree of comfort with uncertainty.

None of this is to say that there is not value or joy to be found in managing the expected. Think of the most regimented people you know. Maybe it's you! The always-on-time, possibly over-scheduled, definitely on-top-of-stuff, no-nonsense type. There is tremendous value in those virtues! But those who find pleasure in the expected often struggle with humor, or at least valuing humor as an equal value to structure. It's not that those of us who value structure have no sense of humor. But if one gets stuck in a cycle of putting forth a disproportionate amount of energy into maintaining the expected, they run the risk of missing out on the joys of the unexpected. Of course, there is equal value in both, but this is a How To Be Happier book, not a How To Get Your Shit Together Book.

We can't always be sitting in the audience of a comedy show, so it's important to find humor in our everyday experiences. Simply allowing yourself different points of view at a given moment is a great way to find humor in the mundane. It can be as overt as realizing it's actually hilarious that you stepped in that puddle as opposed to incredibly annoying. It can be as hidden as realizing the silliness inherent in our particularities—it doesn't have to be devastating that the only open coffee shop near you has only skim milk when you're craving half and half.

That story will be funny later, but it *can* be funny now.

There are times when it feels like you're the punchline in every scene of a sitcom. Just remember: In those moments, there is a laugh track happening somewhere. Allow yourself to join in!

Speaking of joining in, like riding a see-saw, playing checkers, or having sex, laugher is better when you've got company. In fact, a 2012 study found that laughing in groups increases our ability to bond with one another by three hundred percent! Finding someone, or many someones, to laugh with is integral to the experience. It can be sharing everything from small inside jokes to comedy movie night on the couch with your partner. A weekly night of drunken charades with friends. Tickling your infant, telling old stories with college buddies, after-work bitch sessions with co-workers. As E.M. Forster said, "only connect"… but laugh, too. For those who find social bonding more challenging, there are laughter therapy groups available for this express purpose. You'll find space there to be included in the laughter. It is important to remember that laughing *at* someone is antithetical to the experience of laughter. It excludes the person being laughed at, putting more pain than joy into the world as a result.

1.  It seems to me humans have only three things we all agree on:

2.  Alive > Not alive

3.  Pleasure is good

4.  Pain is bad

What we find pleasurable and painful varies, of course, but we all agree that we should chase one and avoid the other while maintaining our "alive" status so we're able to appreciate it all.

Our time is finite in more ways than one, and we all find different things to prioritize. Laughter should be a priority. Laughter isn't something that's an acquired taste or meant only for "certain types" of people. It isn't the way some people find happiness.

Laughter *is* happiness.

Laughter is happiness being expressed in a form so pure and from a place of such presence that it physically overtakes your body. When you are laughing, you are, however briefly, completely connected physically, mentally, and emotionally to your happiness, the very thing that defines "good" for human beings.

Laugh at everything, especially yourself. Manage the expected; find pleasure in calm. But laugh at anything you can. And if you can't find anything to laugh at, there's this '80s movie starring Val Kilmer…

*Peter Grossman is a co-founder of Labyrinth Training, which specializes in animated, interactive corporate trainings. Before moving into the field, he spent more than a decade as a celebrity journalist and liaison to the paparazzi at* Us Weekly*, a natural progression from his college major: music education. Peter lives in Brooklyn with his wife and three children, and laughter is at the center of everything they do.*

---

### Concrete Action

# Smile

A genuine smile is called a Duchenne smile—named after a neurologist named Guillaume Duchenne, who identified the facial muscles that are set into action when we smile spontaneously in reaction to a happy feeling.

But scientists say that producing a fake smile may very well manufacture a happy feeling inside you. So, it's the opposite of how we usually view the connection between happiness and smiling.

---

### Concrete Action

# Find the bright side

Perhaps forcing a smile or laughing can navigate you toward finding the bright side. Just like a comedy takes a dark situation and makes it funny, so can you change your perspective.

You can find beauty anywhere—like a flower growing through a crack in the sidewalk.

*"There are always flowers for those who wish to see them."*

—Henri Matisse

FROM THE DOCTOR'S DESK: LINDSAY S. WEISNER, PSYD

The first time I went to a therapist it was a disaster.

I was twenty-three years old, and I had just gotten out of a mediocre relationship with a miserable ending. I had moved to New York to start grad school, suffered an extremely debilitating injury, and lost my grandfather—all in the span of a few months.

I walked into this therapist's office and started crying before I introduced myself. I told her about my broken heart. I told her about my relationship with my parents. Hell, since I was a first-year grad student at the time, I even managed to find poignant and meaningful connections between my broken heart and my relationship with my parents.

I figured she would be impressed. And pleased. And perhaps silently she would be thrilled that I would soon be a psychologist, since I was so good at connecting the dots.

But when I looked at her, I realized that she looked—sad. She looked really sad. Sad for me, and for what I had been through, and for how I was feeling.

It didn't feel good. I didn't want to go back.

But… she had come highly recommended.

And more importantly, I didn't want to appear *to* be *resistant*.

*Resistant* was a word that seemed to slither off the tongues of all of my professors that first year. There was definitely a Harry Potter, Slytherin, He Who Shall Not Be Named thing going on when someone spoke of a *resistant* patient. A resistant patient isn't ready to help themselves. A resistant patient isn't ready to "do the work of therapy." A resistant patient disagrees with the therapist's suggestions and interpretations. A resistant patient might leave therapy under the guise of not feeling like the therapist was a good fit.

I did not want to think of myself as resistant. And I *absolutely* did not want this therapist to think of me as resistant. So, I certainly wasn't going to be *resistant* and not return for the next session.

I returned to her the following week. I spoke about how strange it was having moved to a new state for graduate school and knowing no one, especially after spending what felt like a significant time with a small group of people during and after college. It was actually kind of lonely.

And again, she looked…sad.

Every word of empathy, every sigh of sympathy, every look that seemed like she felt badly for me—it all added more weight onto the invisible pile of crap and grief that I had been dragging around with me for months.

When I shared my confusion with my husband (and fellow classmate), he pointed out that resistance was a subjective term, and one that could be used incorrectly by the person in power.

Maybe it wasn't that I was resistant, so much as that I didn't feel as if I would benefit from her sympathetic, empathetic, sad-faced approach.

Psychologist Aaron Beck believed that those who suffer from depression are stuck in a so-called cognitive triad of automatic, uncontrollable, negative thoughts. Namely:

1. I feel hopeless

2. I feel helpless

3. Things are never going to get better

I think this is a pretty accurate description of the mindset of depression. And you know what really, truly, absolutely isn't helpful to me when something bad happens? That look on the therapist's face as she says, "Oh, how sad, I'm so sorry that happened to you," and that *tut tut* sound your grandmother used to make escapes from her lips.

You know the look, right? Her pupils enlarge ever so slightly in surprise and perhaps disbelief. The corners of her mouth tilt downward in sadness, and perhaps an expression of some sort of subconscious disapproval. My words—and my experience—have made her feel sad.

The tilt of her head somehow makes me feel like she is grateful that my problems are not hers, in a there-but-for-the-grace-of-God-go-I kind of way.

She didn't do anything wrong. In fact, she is doing what all sweet, kind, well-meaning people do. (Which is probably why I don't spend a lot of time with sweet, kind, well-meaning people.)

I get that this look, those sounds, that gentle pat of my hand—this is all intended to convey comfort and support. But for me, this has always felt like pity. It's as if this type of reaction just further reinforces my cognitive triad, my feelings of hopelessness, helplessness, and the belief—fear—that things will never get better.

These days, I only air my dirty laundry to people who will laugh with me—or even at me—when I am crying. These people, or my People, as I like to think of them, can be across the street or across the country. These are the ones I can call crying at any time of the day or night, and they will find a way for me to end the call laughing. My People are smart and witty and sarcastic and not always fit for public consumption. Which is part of what makes them mine, part of what makes them perfect for me.

When my daughter gets a concussion two days after my son gets rushed to the emergency room, my best friends, my husband, my People are the ones who nod and say, "Of course. You really didn't have anything else going on."

When my cat had to be rushed into life-saving surgery because he had stones that were blocking his bladder and could potentially send him into kidney failure, my People were there. My People giggled and pointed out that by surgically shortening the urethra in order to pass the stones, my male cat was now possibly, technically, a female. Instead of wringing out my hands and worrying while the cat was under the knife, we discussed pronouns and whether we should issue the cat a new birth certificate.

For me, it has always felt better to laugh than to cry.

Laughter releases endorphins, and that good feeling makes me feel *hopeful* that there will be more laughter and more good times in the future.

Comedy is an action, it requires a decision to find the funny and an intellectual effort to do so in a way that is clever and poignant. It's tough to feel *helpless* when you are making a joke. And when your joke makes other people laugh it feels like you have accomplished something. It can't be a coincidence that so many professional comedians have struggled with depression and mental illness.

And what about the third part of the triad, that belief that *things will never get better?*

When I'm laughing with my People instead of crying by myself, it already feels like things have gotten better. Which is a damn good start.

---

It's not where you are outwardly that counts—it's how you view it inwardly.

*"Barn's burned down, now I can see the moon."*

—Zen saying

*"We're all in the gutter, but some of us are looking at the stars."*

—Oscar Wilde

*"There are only two ways to live your life. One is as though nothing is a miracle. The other is as though everything is a miracle."*

—Albert Einstein

---

## Concrete Action

# The power of paws

If you live in a place that allows pets, consider bringing a furry companion into your life. They provide unconditional love and offer you a chance to give love (as important as getting it). Cat or dog, which speaks to you? Why not head down to a shelter and save a life?

If you can't have a furry pet, you can still have paws in your life—and make a difference in theirs. Why not volunteer at a local shelter? Or you can offer to petsit or walk dogs for neighbors or friends.

---

### A NOTE FROM THE EXPERT: CASEY LEE FERRI

Right around the time I graduated from high school, my world began to crumble.

My parents finally put an end to the marriage they had been holding together for as long as I could remember. The stay-at-home mother I had grown up with was suddenly working full time, struggling to keep a roof over our heads. It wasn't long before Mom and I had to move to a new home in a new town. And as if life as I knew it hadn't diminished already, it certainly did when I found that the only aunt I had was forced to go away for some time, leaving behind three children that my mom, grandma, and I had to take in as our own.

As time went on, I began to feel really down. I realized I was struggling with depression and decided I could push through the most difficult feelings by distracting myself with things I enjoyed. I busied myself until I was blue in the face. But enjoyable distractions and busy schedules aren't always good for your mental and physical health.

If you were to ask me my priorities at any point in the last ten years, I would have been quick to list them off with the utmost confidence: health, family and friends, and school/work. In that order. The problem was that I wasn't actually spending time on a lot of my priorities.

The result was that I was in a great place academically, but a bad place personally. I had unhealthy dietary habits, and due to my childhood fear of doctors I had avoided all doctor's appointments for more than ten years. Sure, I was spending a lot of time on schoolwork, but in part it was because I was easily distracted by electronics, making schoolwork an unnecessarily long task. I chose to spend much of my time home in a blanket in front of my television. I communicated with my friends largely through texts.

My sleep was erratic. I often woke up five to six times a night. I was exhausted and overwhelmed and missing out on time with family and friends.

When I realized what I was doing, I felt awful. And the more I engaged in self-defeating activities, the worse I felt.

I decided I needed change. Adopting my dog, Sasha, was the best thing that ever happened to me. Sasha is an extremely quirky, lovable, and energetic dog. It wasn't long before she became my companion, doing everything with me: the beach, daily walks, and outings to the park.

But it didn't take long to notice that Sasha was different from other dogs. When she saw other dogs in the neighborhood or at the dog park, she shied away from them and tried to hide behind me. It seemed like she experienced the same level of anxiety in almost every situation she encountered. Sure, she was cross-eyed and often bumped into walls, but to me, these differences had just made her unique. I was a new mommy, after all, and at first it didn't occur to me that there might be something wrong with her.

And then there was the first seizure. Our vet quickly determined that the seizure was triggered by anxiety and prescribed Sasha Prozac to calm her nerves. The medication dramatically improved her quality of life... for a little while.

Then she began frequently getting sick with parasites from other dogs, causing her hair to fall out, ear infections, digestive issues, and more. We soon learned that Sasha had a rare disease called nodular dermatofibrosis, which produces carcinoma lump growths in her reproductive systems, kidneys, throat, and paws. This past November, Sasha underwent successful surgery for a cluster of lumps in her throat. But our vet warned us that this disease will most likely come back.

It was during that time when I realized all the changes in my life, which had created challenges along with the painful struggle of depression, were nothing in comparison to the pain and fear Sasha was dealing with. And yet, every day my incredible companion woke up with such a sense of life, energy, and strength.

It was incredibly inspiring.

And yet here I was, cutting corners on life.

Without my full devotion to Sasha's medical needs, she would not have been able to survive much longer. And yet with me, Sasha wasn't just living, she was thriving. As her medical needs became more apparent, it became equally apparent that I needed to step up who I was in order to take care of both of us.

Today, Sasha's illness means she can no longer go to the dog park and socialize with other dogs. This prevents me from taking her on long walks. I leave my phone behind to make the walks special. These walks are mandatory for her health and simultaneously beneficial to mine. And without my phone, Sasha and I get to enjoy nature and our time together.

Regardless of Sasha's limitations, the bond we have is unimaginable, and I have never felt such a profound sense of unconditional love in my life. Sure, everything I do with Sasha requires a lot of planning and thought, but this has taught me to appreciate the little things in life, and to break each day into small meaningful pieces instead of just engaging in mindless activities. The sense of companionship, responsibility, and purpose I get from being Sasha's mother brightens every day for me.

It seems like all we ever do is run from activity to activity and obligation to obligation.

Some people shy away from a pet, believing that if they barely have time for themselves, they couldn't possibly have time to care for a pet. And for some people, this may be true. There are always concerns with training and commitment. But finding a service animal or adopting an older trained dog alleviates much of the puppy worries and will do both you and the pet a favor. Luckily, the needs of all pets are not created equal, and this is something to consider before choosing a furry friend.

Training a puppy isn't all fun party tricks. There is more involved than simply teaching him to sit, stay, and roll over. Obedience training, getting your young dog accustomed to walking on a leash, and perhaps the most challenging: toilet training (or housebreaking) are only a few of obstacles involved.

Being a pet owner—a good pet owner—is not easy. But for me, any sacrifices I make while caring for my pet also motivate me to do a better job taking care of myself. And I'm not alone. Research commonly suggests that pet owners have been found to benefit from engaging in higher activity levels than non-pet owners. There are concrete physical benefits associated with pet ownership, like lowered blood pressure and less stress. Pets also appear to reduce the number of visits to the doctor for the owner.

Caring for Sasha forces me to adhere to a schedule, which isn't a bad thing. This schedule actually forces me to care for myself in a more structured, regimented way. For example, when I feed Sasha twice a day, I am reminded that I also need to eat at regular intervals.

Wanting my home to stay clean from shedding can be an extra task. However, because I want a clean house, this is an additional benefit because it gives me a reminder to attend to chores. And lastly, when I let her out the last time each night, I have gotten into the habit of turning off the lights and locking the doors, which is a reminder for me to be winding down and heading to bed at a consistent time. Sasha is a helpless animal and reliant on me for basic needs, which I feel fortunate to have the ability to provide. It reminds me how fortunate I am, and that at times when I feel helpless, there are others I can turn to for support as well—Sasha being one of them.

Pets will fill the void we may feel in our homes and in our hearts. Coming home to someone thrilled to see you and smothering you with love unfortunately is not always a reality. But with a pet, you receive nothing less, each and every time. This presents us with something to look forward to after a long day. We can appreciate a lot from the sense of unconditional love expressed by these creatures. Feeling how loved I am multiple times a day by Sasha reminds me how deserving I am of love, and just this thought helps me love myself.

The companionship and empathy people receive from a loving pet is proven to reduce depression and loneliness. The American Veterinary Association released survey results in 2012 that found nearly fifty percent of participants who considered their pets companions, and ninety-seven percent who talk to their pets daily.

Not only are pets driven by the desire to please you, leading them to spend hours by your side each day, they can also sense when you are sad and want to help you through hugs, kisses, or touching you in some form for comfort. Some individuals may not have the means or willpower to reach out to family and friends right away for a face-to-face interaction, but still desire more. Spending good quality time with a pet through engaging in an activity together or simply spending downtime watching television side by side may become routine to your life. The new sense of connection may urge you to seek out similar forms of interaction in other aspects of life, with other people. For many, this sparks the drive to spend more quality time with loved ones. As these healing experiences become routine parts of a day, pet owners will likely feel themselves growing happier and healthier as a whole.

Overall, giving part of myself to Sasha has made me a better person. Having my priorities aligned with my actions led to a sense of accomplishment. Through helping to care for Sasha, I have also learned to care for myself and other human beings. Most importantly, I have begun to understand that if I do not care for myself first, I will not physically and emotionally have the capacity to care for her.

Both children and adults need to understand that it is so vital to first become the best version of yourself before you plan to present your true self to others. Find things that make you happy, and do them! Make a list of goals; start small and complete them, and when you are ready for some extra special love, adopt a pet. Pets are natural teachers, sharing with us the true image of friendship: loyalty, empathy, kindness. They share with us the ideal form of companionship: social interaction and connection; the true image of health: physical, values, meaning, purpose, play. And lastly, pets offer us unconditional love. All of these are qualities essential for healthy development.

There will be many things you do in your life that will bring you purpose, meaning, and peace. Adopting a pet will give you all three.

So sooner or later, adopt a pet. You will not regret it.

*Casey Lee Ferri is currently a doctoral student at Hofstra University's School-Community PsyD program. After graduation, (the future) Dr. Ferri is interested in working in a forensic mental health setting with law enforcement and other first responders, as well as juvenile offenders. She maintains a (mostly healthy) obsession with her dog, Sasha. CaseyFerri@gmail.com*

# SEEK YOUR HAPPY PLACE

**W**here do you feel happy? Ideally, your answer would be "everywhere". But you wouldn't be reading this if that were the case. Let's examine places, and see where happy speaks to you!

## A Happy Home

As we learned in *The Wizard of Oz*: "There's no place like home."

I think that's why we're so riveted by that movie. It's our search for home—the desire to belong somewhere, even though many of us did not have a happy place to live as children.

The desire to belong to someone, or to somewhere is actually what inspired me to write my novel, *Melt*. It's a flip on Dorothy's mantra about home. What happens when "home" is the worst place to be—upsetting, unsafe, and even terrifying?

We carry our childhood homes in our hearts, and this can be a big roadblock in our search for happy.

Let the past go and find your "now" happy place. It's time to put on your big girl /big boy pants, let your past go, and find the place that can make you happy now.

You can create your own safe place, your own home, or "home" wherever you are!

Even if you can't afford to live in the type of place you think will bring you happiness, you can work with it to inspire and elevate your mood.

> *"Why should we think upon things that are lovely? Because thinking determines life. It is a common habit to blame life upon the environment. Environment modifies life but does not govern life. The soul is stronger than its surroundings."*
>
> —William James

You can turn any environment into an uplifting one! How depends on what elevates you. Perhaps you don't really know what would raise your spirits—maybe you've never thought outside that mental box you've packed yourself in. How exciting—you get to discover what turns your spirit on! Enjoy this process of discovery!

Even if you can't afford to live in the type of place you think will bring you happiness, you can work with it to inspire and elevate your mood.

> *"Look at everything as though you are seeing it either for the first or last time, then your time on earth will be filled with glory."*
>
> —Betty Smith

Take some time to observe the world—your world—in a different way. What are the things that appeal to your mind and senses? Some people, like me, are color-driven. If you're struck by certain colors, use them in your notebook.

*"If you look the right way, you can see that the whole world is a garden."*

—Frances Hodgson Burnett,
The Secret Garden

---

### Selene's Purple Story

 *I am extremely color-driven. Purple is my color, and when my home was destroyed by Hurricane Sandy, I decided that I was going to start over and do it my way—by incorporating purple in all different shades! My walls, doors, porch, shutters, curtains... all varying shades of purple, from light to dark. And I love it! Even my steps are purple, and I used chalk paint so I could write quotes on them. (Another major passion of mine is collecting quotes, which you may have noticed in this book!)*

---

*"Home is where the happy stuff is!"*

—Selene Castrovilla

Now that you know what makes you environmentally happy, consider how you can go and get it! Read through this next section, and take more notes about which suggestions speak to you. Don't rush to act. Wait until you read the concrete actions at the end.

If you love a certain color, why not bring in things with that color? They don't have to be expensive, or even new. You can find trinkets and home goods of any color in thrift stores. How about a bright linen draped over that beat-up coffee table, or even over a storage crate or cardboard box? How about a cozy blanket you can cuddle up with?

If you like to play around in the kitchen, try some gadgets or new (to you) plates.

If you love to read, how about buying a pile of used books? I especially love books people have written notes in. It's so interesting to see what spoke to them. It's like the shared experience of being in a book club!

If you love plants, plan on acquiring at least one that appeals to you. When you do get it, name it. Speak to it. If you're worried about killing it (as I have done with every indoor plant I've owned), get a cactus or a bamboo plant. It's very hard to kill them! Or you could even buy a fake plant, if you just like the ambience.

If, like me, you find quotes inspirational, you can purchase some picture frames and either type up and print your favorite quotes or handwrite them with colorful markers.

If you like nature from an observational standpoint, hang up environmental pictures that speak to you.

If you like sports, hang up sports pictures or memorabilia. You can even put a baseball next to your coffee maker or in your fruit bowl… you get the idea!

If you're quirky, seek the most ridiculous knick-knacks you can find that will bring a smile to your face every time you look at them. I have sock monkeys in my bathroom and a row of rubber ducks in my kitchen. (Get it? All of my ducks are in a row.) I also have funny and satirical greeting cards framed.

If you're sentimental, surround yourself with things that will prompt happy memories—photos, ticket stubs, or anything that brings you back to a treasured moment. (Guess what, I am into this too! I have pictures of my sons all over my house!)

You may not be able to pick the ideal location, but for very little investment you can create your happy place wherever you are.

*"Beautiful things comfort; they bring a real clarity and ease. We have to continue to make our environments beautiful—it's sort of like a prayer."*

—Anjelica Huston

The thing I want you to embrace is that your environment is something you can experiment with, and you have the power to "own it"—even if you rent. It's a reflection of you, and it also reflects "into" you. If it makes you unhappy, you will be unhappy inside.

*"Dwell in possibility."*

—Emily Dickinson

I invite you to literally dwell in possibility. Make your home a place where anything is possible, and happiness will always be there.

# Work Environment

The place where you work is, in a way, your second home.

What do you surround yourself with for those eight hours a day?

If you sit at a desk, does it display things that make you happy?

If you have a job "on the go" you're luckier—your environment isn't stagnant. It's up to you to let wherever you go on your day's journey spark inspiration—and this is something we're going to be working on. If you use a vehicle, hang something happy from your rearview mirror. Put a funny bobblehead on the dashboard. Do something to make your car your happy place! I have gemstones (purchased in a metaphysical supply store) in the little dish between the seats.

If you take public transportation, look at things in a new light. Find unexpected objects or interesting people. Consider graffiti or ads from a different angle. Everything can be seen in a positive way—every place can be your happy place as you pass through it.

Did you know that the word "hobo" is thought to come from the phrase "homeward bound"? A hobo makes every place his home, since he doesn't have a permanent one. I invite you to think like a hobo and make yourself at home in every transient environment you pass through. Because your real home is inside you. Your body is a mobile home transporting your mind and soul.

If you work in an indoor environment where you don't have your own designated space, perhaps you can wear something that makes you happy—a bracelet or a button. Consider funky nail polish, a novelty tie, or a cool pinky ring. And keep something in your bag that makes you happy.

And what about creating a "happy common space?" At a school I teach in, a faculty member took a vote on theme and collected donations for sprucing up the teachers' lounge. The result is a relaxing and inviting environment all the teachers and staff enjoy.

# Outpost Happy Place

So far, we have discussed places where you live or work—but you can also find an "outpost happy place"—a neighborhood happy hang-out! Writers are known for finding a cozy coffee shop and hunkering down for hours near an outlet. Sports fans will likely find a happy spot in a sports-themed restaurant or bar (sometimes you can find places themed after a particular team, or people who all love a team hang out there.) Really, the possibilities are endless as to where you can seek outpost happy places!

Museums are enlightening and invigorating. Art prompts your brain to think in different directions than your norm, and that raises your spirit with purpose. Do you have a favorite artist? As I mentioned earlier, mine is Claude Monet. There's a huge room at New York's Metropolitan Museum of Art devoted to Monet's paintings, complete with benches for contemplation. I love sitting there, staring into the dreamy paintings, each telling its own story—or prompting me to tell its story.

*"It's on the strength of observation and reflection that one finds a way. So we must dig and delve unceasingly."*

—Claude Monet

Yes, a happy place can inspire you. I've used the Met's Monet room in two of my novels!

*Melt*, a book I call a brutal romance, is told in two voices. First, Dorothy tells how she took her boyfriend Joey to the Monet room:

*Then I took him upstairs, to the paintings.*

*To my favorite place in the museum, and possibly in the world.*

*To the Monet room, a place where you could actually be among some of the finest works of Claude Monet, who was in my opinion the greatest of the Impressionist painters. Monet was infatuated with gardens and water and often depicted both. He created stunning pastel-colored, dream-like portraits of nature.*

*This room is my sanctuary.*

*We circled the room slowly, weaving through people, taking everything in.*

*The last painting was my favorite. Bursts of lavender water lilies floating on an ethereal pond. I turned to tell Joey how much I loved it, but stopped when I saw his face. I didn't have to tell him—he felt the same way. He was mesmerized, steeped in thought. It was as though he was trying to figure out how to enter the painting. Or maybe, somehow, he had.*

*After a while he turned to me, smiled that little smile. "Thanks," he said.*

*I took his hand, led him to the bench in the center of the room. Surrounded by beauty, we sat.*

*We sat crooked, his denim-covered knees touching mine in grey tights.*

*I felt this tingling through my legs and I inched closer into him, into his arms.*

*God, I felt so safe in those arms.*

*So, so safe.*

*Then he kissed me.*

Then I juxtaposed it with Joey in the home where his family is abused by his father, using his memory with Dorothy (also called "Doll") in the Monet room as an escape.

*Now Doll comes into my head.*

*Me and Doll with all them paintings water water everywhere.*

*Sweet sweet Doll oh god I can taste her lips they're like oxygen pure oxygen a dose of fresh air they're hope she tastes like hope.*

*For the first time I'm not hopeless.*

*We're kissing I'm hoping and the room turns slow all them paintings swirl around us they take us in.*

*We're gliding through them lily pads swimming we swim we're breathing underwater we blend we mix we melt right into them whirling bursts of colors where everything's connected where everything belongs where everything's right.*

*The world's so right finally it all makes sense but then I quit.*

*I quit I quit I quit kissing her I push her away I let her float back to the surface.*

*It ain't right swimming with her using her to breathe like that.*

*I can't I can't I can't take the chance of dragging her down to the murk with me.*

*She don't belong at the bottom of the pond she don't belong here in my kitchen.*

*I can't let her be here even just in my mind she might get muddy.*

So you see how I make use of a setting as my inspiration. With the Monet room, it's instinctive. It keeps coming back. I used it again, in a way that's both different and similar, in my women's novel *Love the Ones You're With*:

*We sit like that for a while. Our quiet is punctured by the voices in the hall. Everyone is still gathered at the scene of the crime. Through the window, I can see the top of the Metropolitan Museum. It's my favorite. I used to take the kids there, to the Egyptian section. It has a pyramid, or at least part of one.*

*Luke says, "I guess this party wasn't a good idea."*

*I don't say anything. I'm thinking about the museum. My favorite spot in there —actually, one of my favorite places anywhere—is the Monet room. An area devoted to Monet's impressionism. You can sit on a bench and look at his work for as long as you want.*

*I used to sit there and wish I could be inside those paintings, in Monet's thoughtful, swirling world. Where nothing could be bad, you could just be in this peaceful place where no one would hurt you.*

*"I'm sorry I upset you, Miranda, " Luke says.*

*"Did you ever go to the Monet room?"*

*He looks confused. "Excuse me?"*

*"Across the street, in the museum. There's this room filled with paintings by Monet."*

*Now he's looking at me like I'm a patient in a mental ward, speaking in non sequiturs. "Um, no. Haven't been there. Sounds…nice?"*

*"You can sit on a bench for as long as you like."*

*"Okaaay…Would you like me to go with you one day?"*

*"You would sit with me there?"*

*"Sure."*

*And for one moment I get excited, at the thought of sharing my special room with someone who wants to be there with me.*

*But then I realize it's not going to happen. He'll say anything right now to calm me down. He might even think he means it. But he'll never do it. The dream isn't really in the paintings. The dream is believing in people.*

"But I'm not a writer!" you protest.

But you are. You're the author of *your* story. Just as my characters fall into circumstances they can't control, so have you. We can't plan out our lives perfectly, but we can pick the setting we choose to be in during our leisure time. And we can make sure that setting is a happy place.

I know I've thrown a lot at you here, and I don't want you to feel overwhelmed! So, here's what you can do right now to get started:

## Concrete Action

# Embrace Nature as an Outpost Happy Place

Here are three huge reasons to turn to nature—and the first two are purely scientific.

## Sunshine

*"Turn your face to the sun and the shadows fall behind you."*

—Unknown

Serotonin is a chemical in our brains that significantly boosts happiness. In fact, most antidepressants focus on serotonin production.

When we spend time outdoors exposing ourselves to the sun for at least twenty minutes, the UV sunrays we absorb promote serotonin pro-duction. Hence, the sun is nature's antidepressant! (Just make sure to wear organic sunscreen.)

If you ever wondered why you feel sadder in the winter, part of the reason may well be that you don't go outside as much, or for as long.

# Fresh Air

*"And this new air was so delicious, and all his old life seemed so far away, that he forgot for a moment about his bruises and his aching muscles."*

—C.S. Lewis, The Horse and His Boy

The second reason also relates to serotonin. When you breathe in fresh air, your serotonin production is again increased!

# Nature's Lessons

*"Look deep into nature and you will understand everything better."*

—Albert Einstein

Nature's lessons could fill a whole book! Here are some of the things you'll gain insights in:

**Interdependence**—Buddha learned to appreciate interdependence by sitting under a tree.

**Patience**—Nature never rushes!

**Adaptation**—Nature adjusts to any conditions.

**Beauty**—So many magnificent colors! So many interesting shapes! So many wondrous things! Perhaps nature will redefine beauty for you.

*"If the stars should appear but one night every thousand years how man would marvel and adore."*

—Ralph Waldo Emerson

**Resilience**—Nature recovers from setbacks.

**Stability and reassurance**—Everything in nature works as it should, without worry.

**Embrace simplicity**—Nature doesn't overcomplicate.

*"To find the universal elements enough; to find the air and the water exhilarating; to be refreshed by a morning walk or an evening saunter…to be thrilled by the stars at night; to be elated over a bird's nest or a wildflower in the spring—these are some of the rewards of the simple life."*

—John Burroughs

And of course, nature inspires.

*"The richness I achieve comes from nature, the source of my inspiration."*

—Claude Monet

## A NOTE FROM THE EXPERT: NICOLE GLASSMAN

Several years ago, I was a slave to the monotony of life, slowly being strangled by my own schedule and my endless ambition. I was trying to run my holistic health company, and in an attempt to lessen my load, I somehow thought starting to produce a healthy baked product was a good idea.

For two years I struggled to get this product off the ground, only to realize that this was far from my passion. I spent countless dollars, endless hours, not to mention sleepless nights, baking in my own kitchen, all in an attempt to get this product "just right." The process was, at best, draining.

When my friends, family, and clients would ask me how my new and exciting project was going, I tried to avoid answering. The truth was, this project was going nowhere. I was officially miserable, but afraid to throw in the towel and admit defeat.

It wasn't until I spent the day with my cousin and my dear friend in nature that I was able to gain some perspective. Being surrounded by trees rooted me to my truth, and I finally had the fortitude to admit to my internal battle. After an hour of tears, I found that being in nature allowed me to connect to my vulnerability and find an inner stillness. I finally had the clarity I needed. And there was power in admitting it was time to let go.

This experience shed light on a giant void and helped me to uncover the real truth: I thought I had been searching for a business opportunity that would give me more time and freedom to play and enjoy life, but what I was really seeking was connection.

My routine life had been entirely disconnected—robotic and solitary. I worked alone, in New York City, surrounded by concrete. I desperately needed to soak in the sun. I craved greenery and trees and water. I missed connecting with animals. I felt alone and needed to find like-minded women to talk with about business and life. I wanted to eat at a slow pace, and enjoy my meals, and not feel like every day was a fire drill. I wanted to feel present and creative and alive with possibilities.

I decided to fill my own voids and that of my clients, who echoed similar sentiments, by creating a program that provides people with the tools they need to feel connected.

Studies show that being near trees can lower cortisol, blood pressure, improve the nervous system function, and alleviate our overall stress response. There are also studies that show that exposure to soil boosts your mood and your immunity.

I, too, feel transformed when I am immersed in nature, so I decided to create retreats where nature was center stage. I have been running my Mindful Mosaic Women's Retreats for seven years now. Each one is held in a spectacular natural setting, such as on a gorgeous lake in New York's Finger Lakes region, or on the stunning beaches of Tulum, Mexico, or the tranquil farms of Vermont and New York's Hudson Valley. I offer boating, hiking, and forest bathing (nature walks in the forest), yoga on a velvety green lawn, a visit with the mischievous and often hilarious goats on a farm, a chance to experience horses and their healing benefits, along with simple pleasures like building sandcastles near the waves. These retreats are designed to help women play, dig deep, explore, and find peace.

Nature can help you to find balance, and the effects of nature can be especially powerful during times of change. A few years ago, I lost my mother unexpectedly. A loss of this magnitude creates tears in the seams of the family lining. Everyone handles grief in their own way, and although I was suffering too, I was consumed with making things feel normal, which is impossible. So not only was I dealing with the grief, I was also struggling with the stress of making sure family members stayed connected, and that no one went silent for too long. So, when the dust settled, my instinct was once again to run away into nature. I spent the week alone at a hotel on the beach. But this wasn't enough for me. I needed to explore my emotions and disappear for a moment, but feel like people were there when I was ready to share. I wanted to combine nature with a community that would understand what I was experiencing. Building on my own needs, I expanded my program to create space for people who needed to heal from something, perhaps a transition in a woman's life—a move, job change, a death, a divorce, or even a new marriage. Now I offer exercises to help people going through exactly this, and I even include some time to play in the dirt!

The need to feel grounded often arises during times of change. Nature can be a powerful conduit for feeling safe and embracing vulnerability in new ways. I find that even introverts freely share on my retreats because nature calms the nervous system and serves as a security blanket. Combining nature with a beautiful community can be so powerful!

My last retreat was magical. It was held on a beautiful goat farm in Vermont. There were ten dynamic women whose ages ranged from twenty-seven to seventy. Their age differences were vast, but their stories were equivalent. They were there because they had lost their sense of joy and purpose; they had lost their center. Their next steps were unknown and full of fear, and their lives were too chaotic to reflect or to create change. At the end of the program I had asked them to fill out an evaluation. The question was, "Why did you choose this particular retreat?" Once again, the answers were identical: They wanted to feel connected to nature.

Nature, in its quiet way, helps you to find perspective. It restores the body with its gentle breeze, nurtures with its blanketed forests, and quiets the mind with its soothing seas. It allows you to be present to feel, to see, and to hear. And when the mind is still and the senses are open, the answers you are seeking are loud and clear.

*Nicole Glassman is a holistic nutritionist, blogger, public speaker, founder of Mindful Health, and the creator of the Mindful Mosaic Program and product line. She has hosted numerous workshops and retreats that empower people to live with passion and purpose. Nicole completed her Masters in food studies at New York University and her Holistic Health Counseling Certificate at the Institute of Integrative Nutrition. She is currently working on her first book. Nicole can be reached at nicole@mindfulhealth.biz.*

## Concrete Action

# Creating your home happy place

Go over your notes of things that make you happy from the beginning of this step. Make a list of things you could do without much effort to brighten up your environment(s) to your particular tastes. (Using my suggestions as a starting off point—but heading wherever you'd like!)

Pick one area from your list to focus on and head to a thrift store or some other store that appeals to you. You can also shop online. Your goal is to find one item that will make your environment happy to you. (If you find more, so be it!) Repeat this exercise once a week, until your happy place(s) feels just right to you.

Bonus action: Share your happy home vibes!

Another way to create your happy place is to invite people you like and enjoy to visit. Perhaps you have co-workers or people who share a hobby or interest. I like to be around other writers, and when I have them over for some wine, cheese, and conversation, I'm so happy! If your friends are far away, consider video chatting with them on a regular basis. A visual seems to work better than a phone call for me, but hearing voices on a conference call may work for you. We live in an amazing age for technology—there's no reason we can't use it to create our happy atmosphere.

Concrete Action

# Creating a happy work space

Bring in one thing to keep on your desk that will always bring a smile to your face.

Concrete Action

# Finding your outpost happy place

Take a purposeful stroll around the neighborhood for a potential outpost happy place. Then try it out! Keep an open mind—if you're like me, you need to settle into a place and get used to it. You may find a place to be happy for a whole other reason than you thought it would be. Maybe you've found a few potential places—try them all! You may want to alternate your happy places, or you may want to ultimately settle into one special hangout.

Bonus action: Invite friends to your hangout! (To make new friends, see the concrete actions in Step Three.)

# SURROUND YOURSELF WITH SHINING, HAPPY PEOPLE

e need people. And yet, we have become afraid to reach out to each other.

> *"If we have no peace, it is because we have forgotten that we belong to each other."*
>
> —Mother Teresa

It's ironic that in the age of social media, which is supposed to help people come together, many of us have lost our sense of belonging. I think technology has made us more troubled and confused about relating. It's a murky, endless sea, which many of us feel lost in.

There are ways to find like-minded people on social media. I'm far from an expert, but you can start with searching hashtags or looking for groups dedicated to your interests.

People often complain about the viciousness they encounter on social media. But your social media is totally under your control, because you can block, unfriend, or unfollow people who upset you. The worst thing you can do is argue or engage with them. This just drags you down. Find the upbeat people—those who are always looking for another way to solve a problem, who want to congratulate and support one another, who inspire.

You are the company you keep.

*"The key is to keep company only with people who uplift you, whose presence calls forth your best."*

—Epictetus

Upbeat people will raise your spirits, so they are important to seek in real life as well. You deserve to hang out with the smiling and laughing people. But remember to laugh and smile with them. There's an old saying, "No one likes a Debbie Downer." That's because a "downer" brings down the whole mood. Perhaps in the past you've felt like a downer, and that no one "fun" would want to hang around with you. But that was then, this is now. You don't have to be a downer! (See Step One, and repeat actions as needed.) This is the new you—you just have to believe it. Once you do that, the shining, happy people will come to you! Accept that you deserve their friendship, and share your friendship with them. Trust me, this will all come together naturally—just don't fight it!

The next part of this equation is to find your tribe—not just *any* shining, happy people, but the specific shining, happy people for you.

You must hang out with people who have similar interests. This can mean anything, to anyone. Look for people who have similar:

careers

passions

hobbies

recreational interests

music

religious/spiritual beliefs

*"Tell me with whom you associate, and I will tell you who you are."*

—Johann Wolfgang von Goethe

Like-minded people will make you happy! You'll be excited to share your enthusiasm and have people to talk with about the thing(s) you love!

*"Your enlightenment depends on the company you keep."*

—Woodrow Wilson

*"It is better to be alone than in bad company."*

—George Washington

In other words: Be your own shining, happy person! Eventually, good company will gravitate to you!

Always remember to convey happiness! Don't look for it in others, but rather, share it with them. (Some briefly, and some steadily—the choice is yours!)

### Selene's Story

*My life took an amazing upswing when I found my first writers group. People who shared my passion for words! I call a gathering of writers a "vortex of creativity." It's not only about companionship, but it also lifts my passions and spurs me on. This raises the vibrational harmony of the universe. The more we surround ourselves with people who share our joys, the more joy rises into the universe.*

## Concrete Action

# Four choices for friendship

1. If you want to make new, local friends with a shared interest, consider Meetup. You can join one and perhaps find a happy place where the group meets, or suggest *your* happy place as another meeting place. You can also create a Meetup group of your own. Or check out what kind of networking exists in your area, either in-person or virtual.

2. If you can't find a way to connect in-person, you can join a Facebook group and connect with people with the same interests (while you're in your happy place!).

3. Stay in touch with your old friends through social media—as long as you continue to feel simpatico to their views/interests. But disengage if you're no longer in alignment! You can also e-mail, phone, or even traditionally mail them. Imagine the smile you can bring to a face by sending a cute card or postcard just to say "hi."

4. If you've been a loner at work or school, it's not too late to reach out. I used to feel like an outsider at school—like there was an invisible wall between me and the other kids, and I could only observe them. This was all in my mind! When I reconnected with them as an adult, I learned that they liked me, but didn't think that I liked them! Approach the people you feel a vibe with. Soon, you'll be one of the gang.

# ACCEPT PEOPLE FOR WHO THEY ARE

*"When someone shows you who they are, believe them."*

—Maya Angelou

Y ou must let go of the idea that people will change. Most won't. Ever.

Instead, be grateful for who they are now and for the unique gifts they bring to you.

This includes family and friends.

I learned this from Dr. Daniel Silver, my chiropractor. When I complained that some people had given no gifts except for pain, Dr. Silver said something wild:

*"Thank the people who have hurt you, for they have allowed you to grow."*

*What?*

Thank someone for *hurting me?*

But once I considered Dr. Silver's words, I realized that some of my greatest growth did come from these people—because I had to find a way past the obstacles and pain. Of course, I don't think he meant to literally thank them—though it might be interesting to see their reactions if I did. I thanked them in a more universal way, acknowledging that they had carried me to a higher point in my journey.

This was *not* easy. But wow, it felt great once I did it.

## The Ties That Bind

It's one thing to accept someone peripheral in your life as who they are—a co-worker or acquaintance, for instance. You have no real, emotional ties with them. Friends are harder, because we have "let them in," perhaps relying on them for intimacy and caring we never otherwise received, only to be disappointed. Family is the toughest, due to our complex histories together.

We may have spent hours, days, months, years trying to get something from a person of which they are just not able to give. This could be—and often is—a parent.

We are not to blame for wanting to get the thing or things we never received from our parents. When we were children, we could not even translate into words that hole we felt in our hearts. As adults, perhaps we've made it our mission to obtain that thing we feel we deserved—love, appreciation, affirmation that we *mean* something. But how could the person who let us down for all those years suddenly have the wherewithal to rise to the occasion? Sure, this happens onscreen—in the movies and on TV. And maybe you can really have a conversation and express your pain, anger, and hurt at their failings. But there's no "fade out" to a happy ending in real life. Your parent may apologize and even appear to want to make amends. And that's wonderful. But don't hold your breath waiting for an actual change in them after that. It's not you—it's them.

When I expressed to Dr. Silver that my childhood made me feel worthless, he told me:

***"Your parents are not God."***

You parents have no reflection on you, and they cannot impact you unless you let them.

Let it go!

And I will admit that I enjoy the Disney song, too.

Try letting it go. I did.

This is essential for you to find happy. It applies to all relatives—grandparents, siblings, aunts, and uncles too. All imperfect humans, struggling to find their way.

If you were the victim of abuse, I implore you to seek professional help, if you haven't yet. You can get through this step and find your happy—but you need assistance.

---

## A NOTE FROM THE EXPERT: MAX GREY

As a child, my life was perfect. Or at least, it seemed to be to anyone on the outside looking in. But what went on behind closed doors took a lot out of me, physically and emotionally.

I was around three years old when my parents divorced. The divorce was messy—both my mother and father refused to find a way to get along for the sake of me, and although everyone involved tried their best, I still found myself stuck in the middle. I felt like a rag doll or a punching bag, desperately trying to please both of my parents. When I was fourteen, I was the victim of sexual abuse. The perpetrator was someone I knew, which made it all the more confusing.

I learned from an early age to organize and categorize my environment in ways that were more logical than emotional. I learned to be sensitive to other people's emotions and energies, and I was wary of the dynamics between people. I had to be.

Ultimately, this made me a keen observer, and I always wanted to learn more about the people I was around. I watched and wondered and asked questions, not out of politeness or curiosity, but because it felt like I needed to know. I needed to know all of the grit, the deep, inner thoughts, the history and shaping of these people. I needed to know how they related to the world on a soul level, not just the surface where things appeared to be pretty and nice and happy. I needed to see every single layer.

I was at the very young age of six when I realized that most of what we see is pre-determined by expectations. Seeing how differently my parents acted in the public eye as compared to at home is what made me come to this realization. My friends and neighbors saw what they wanted to see, what they expected to see, based on where we lived and what I looked like. I also realized that most people worked hard to create this façade of who they were, all in an attempt to control how other people saw them. This scared the shit out of me. Who was safe—and who wasn't—if most people were polishing their armor of pretend and then presenting this to the world as their truth?

I refused to fall for this façade of "happy" and "everything is fine, at all times." I wanted to see with my heart, rather than my eyes. I wanted to "see" actual feelings and emotions. Even the ones of anger, sadness, guilt, or fear. The emotions society had conditioned us not to expose outward. I wanted to take experiences and interactions and hold them in my hand, connect with people in the ways they were shaped. I craved so much for some sort of tangible process with human experience. One that was not my own, but felt similar. Still imagery was the only way to even come close to manifesting such a thing.

On my seventh birthday, my mother and stepfather gave me a Polaroid camera. And I began to photograph everything. Especially things that the average person wouldn't even think of photographing.

One day I took a picture of one of the dog beds. I grew up with dogs, cats, and horses. My mother and stepfather were dog and horse trainers and devoted a lot of their time volunteering with the SPCA as well. To this day, I can still remember every single crease, stain, and even smell of that dog bed. I remember the yellow stain in the corner of the Polaroid picture of that dog bed, from shaking it too hard to get it to develop faster. It was authentic. It was part of my world.

Another time, when my little brother was almost two years old, I took a picture of him standing in his crib, hysterically crying. I vividly remember the sound of his crying, what he was wearing, and the room that was pitch black until I turned on the lights. I remember that there were no parents in sight. I can't remember why my parents weren't around or why, exactly, my brother was crying.

It is the honesty of this image that sticks with me. And the story as told by that picture seemed to speak for itself. There was really no need for context or an outcome.

When I had my first child, I suffered from severe postpartum depression. With all of the stuff I went through as a child, I don't think I ever fully understood the idea of safety in my own life. And now here I was, struggling to keep another life safe. Also, I was young, and I was one of the first people in my circle of friends to have children. It felt… like I was alone.

One day, I remembered that Polaroid picture of my brother. It ignited something inside of me. It was so much more than just a picture. It was the entire experience around it. The emotion that image evoked in me. The ability to be able to go back to that very moment over and over again.

I began to pick up my camera more and more. And through the view from the camera lens, I found a way to cope. To be honest with myself. To look at life around me and document it. It was a healing of sorts.

And this time, as an adult, I had several healthy relationships that pushed me to turn this coping mechanism into something more: my business.

At the time, I never really viewed any of what I was so drawn to in photography, as something related to my childhood or trauma, or patterns of survival. However, based on how I shoot, and what I shoot, and the feelings that come up for me, how could I not? My life's work is focused on the birth of babies, on families in their very own environment, the unapologetic ways of children and women. All of which are honest, raw, vulnerable, and unique.

As a child, I felt isolated and lost. My Polaroid camera was my way to escape, and my way to feel safe. As an adult, I took the pain from my post-partum depression and channeled it into this business, this passion, that I am lucky enough to share with the world. My photography is more than my business; it has also become my means of connection and a conduit to stay present in the moment—even the difficult ones.

*Max Grey is a photographer, writer, and doula from New York, as well as a mother of two little girls. She graduated college with a degree in English and shortly after opened up her photography business in 2010, where she combines her love of writing with her love of photography to document the world of human connection for people and families. She started her birth/postpartum doula career three years ago, where she continues to support, write about, and photograph these times to create a tangible, healing, and connected process for the families she works with. You can find her on Facebook at facebook.com/maxgreyartist; @maxgreyphotog on Instagram; and at www.maxgreyart.com.*

# Partners

Why do we stay with people who are incompatible with us?

For many, it's in the hope that they will change.

After all, they have good qualities, and/or they take care of *some* of our needs.

But if a partnership isn't totally right, you must recognize that it will likely never be right. It is what it is, because your partner is who he or she is. If you choose to stay, accept this and embrace your partner's imperfections. After all: you, being human, have some too! Or, if you feel like you just can't be happy with this person as is, leave. I would advise not staying together for the sake of the children, because exhibiting an unhappy marriage/parenting model is not in their best interests. And kids can tell when you're unhappy!

## FROM THE DOCTOR'S DESK: LINDSAY S. WEISNER, PSY.D

We all have that special someone who we just can't seem to shake. It's usually a lover, but a friend can break your heart, too. If any of the following sound like a song you have sung oh-so-many times before, maybe it's time for you to break that pattern and cut the toxic friend, lover, or fun boy out of your life.

### *"He's just not my type. The guys I date are usually… different."*

It's very romantic to believe that you will somehow know when you find the right person. That this guy you dreamt of when you were watching *The Little Mermaid* and listening to the soundtrack of some John Hughes movie and standing in line to see *Rent* for the first time… that this ideal guy in your ideal adulthood would be ideally standing beside you.

And now, here you are, and you have grown up in so many ways—I mean, come on, John Cusack was kinda stalker-y in his films and don't even get me started on what the #MeToo movement would have thought about

Judd Nelson's characters—and yet you are still holding onto that ideal image of what your partner *should* be like.

So, you date. But if he isn't tall enough or his legs are too skinny.... If she has never heard of Monty Python or doesn't have that sexy foreign accent that makes your toes curl....

Most of us definitely have a type. Possibly all of us. It's not inherently bad. After all, sexual attraction is absolutely crucial for a healthy relationship—both short term and long term.

But if you are always waiting for the sparks to fly at the first hello, or your "type" to appear as a match in your Tinder profile, you are going to miss out on some really good guys.

You are going to miss out on the "right" guy for you because he is a few inches shorter than your usual type. You are going to miss out on the guy for you because he didn't make your thighs tremble the first time you were introduced to him. Yet who knows—your thighs might have trembled like an earthquake the second time.

What is your type? How rigidly do you adhere to this type that hasn't brought you happiness so far? How long have you had this image of your ideal mate yet subsequently been disappointed by the guys that fit this type?

You should really be curious about this "type" by which you're so restricted.

Is the man of your dreams tall, dark, and handsome? Are you a boobs guy? An ass man? Maybe you only condescend to a date with a guy who has a square jawline, an even scruff, and is six feet or taller.

These physical characteristics do offer distinct evolutionary advantages. If you think back to the caveman days, a larger mate would be better able to keep his family safe and a taller man could reach food on the higher branches of the trees. And, duh, physical attractiveness is a reflection of health. So, if you are attracted to a guy that is pretty to look at (and who offers a subconscious, subliminal bonus of healthier genes for your offspring), what's the negative?

Not a lot.

And you know the whole boobs versus butt debate?

Many of the physical characteristics that make a woman attractive or desirable are signs of sexuality and virility. Large lips and womanly curves all point to the ability to procreate, which means successfully passing on your partner's genes. Passing on genes leads to creating a larger family, and a larger family hopefully means more allies during an attack.

Another interesting, biologically-based preference? Xenophobia and racism.

Humans are no different than other animals. Inherently, our survival depends on fearing those who are different than us. That which is familiar seems safer, and our survival depends on our safety. Although I would like to imagine that we, as humans, are more complex than our furrier friends who may walk on four feet instead of two, the fact is that a certain amount of fear is simply a survival skill.

This type of man that you cling to and swear by yet has left you disappointed so many times in the past? That's just a different form of xenophobia and racism. Which might explain why sticking to your type is a shitty idea. What makes sense in terms of evolutionary biology does not necessarily make sense in terms of what will make *you* happy.

### *"He's just not my type. The guys I date are usually… different."*

No. No, they are not.

Healthy relationships are supposed to make you feel better about who you are.

The right person for you is the person who points out that your snoring is kind of cute. The right person for you is the person who will remind you that even though you have always hated that little bump on your nose, that bump is actually a funny reminder of when six-year-old you was so stubborn and self-assured that you decided to teach yourself to roller skate on a cobblestone driveway.

A healthy relationship does not make you fearful if you see your partner and your best friend talking.

A healthy relationship does not leave you wondering why he takes so damn long to call you back. A healthy relationship does not leave you wondering why your relationship is still undefined after six months of dating.

The guy you get naked with, repeatedly, is supposed to be nice to you.

It should be exciting that he loves you, not that he leaves you hanging.

### *"Why is he doing this to me?"*

He isn't doing this *to you*. He is doing this *for him*.

Does your ex text that he misses you but then fails to follow up on plans? I'm sure your gaggle of girls are quick to jump to your aid and fire accusations that he is sending you mixed signals.

Your ex reaches out to you because he misses you. Or, at least, he misses knowing that someone out there in the world loves him. He reaches out to make himself feel better. Kind of like the guy version of self-care. But that doesn't mean he loves you. If he did love you, he wouldn't reach out to you just because he felt needy or lonely. He would give you the space to move on.

Does your boyfriend, husband, or partner promise to change only to continue doing the same things you have fought about for years? He spent your wedding rehearsal dinner at the bar watching a basketball game instead of greeting the loved ones who had traveled so far to celebrate with you both. Or his weekly happy hour with the boys from work has turned into an all-nighter that leaves you stuck picking up the pieces that evening and the following morning as well. Or he promises to start eating healthy and exercising more but you're constantly finding the remnants of junk food hidden in the garbage can outside your home.

He is choosing his habit over your happiness together. His actions are sending you a clear message that *he* is more important than *you*. He places more importance on his temporary pleasure than on a future with you.

Does he cheat on you? Repeatedly? And leave you wondering why he keeps hurting you like this?

Guess what? It's not about you. It's about him and what he wants. Maybe his father was an adulterer or Mommy always neglected him, and he constantly seeks out female attention to make up for what he lacked in childhood. Maybe his bruised ego constantly needs to be stroked by numerous different hands. Maybe he is selfish or narcissistic or has a deadly fear of commitment.

None of that matters. None.

What matters is that he chooses his needs over yours. He chooses his perverse version of self-care over preserving your heart. He chooses to do things for him that he knows will hurt you. Repeatedly.

And you? You stick around and let him do this. Repeatedly.

Maybe it's time to find someone who does things for you, rather than to you.

---

# Children

When they're little, they're so darn cute! But kids grow up, and sometimes we butt heads. It would behoove us to realize that our view of the world is not the only view, and that our children may see things in a totally different way. We may guide them, and protect them, and influence them—but we can't change them. Embrace and nurture their quirks, and accept that they may not want to be the lawyer, doctor, or artist that you imagined they would be. Try seeing the world through the eyes of your child, and you'll discover a whole new perspective.

When your child is grown, you have the choice to be in their life or not. It may not seem like a choice, but it is. Once again, you cannot change them or make them see things your way. Is it really that important to be "right"? How about just "being happy" in each other's company?

---

## A NOTE FROM THE EXPERT: DR. NILOO DARDASHTI

In my practice, I often see mothers of all ages who, at some point or another, feel stuck and/or disconnected from their own identities and passions. It is often a very similar story in a nutshell: Woman wanted baby; woman gave birth to baby or babies; and somewhere along the line, woman realized that she was so focused on her child that she forgot what it was that she wanted to do with—or for—herself.

The act of having children is one through which we transform and learn from tremendously. The joys, perils, and love that are born along with your child are mind-blowing and sometimes unexpected.

But, practically speaking, it also takes up a lot of time and energy. And before you know it, being a parent can take up all of the space you have—or had—in your own life.

Unless you work hard to maintain some space of your own, to maintain some time and space for you, it's easy for Mom to get carried away and forget about herself.

Eventually, despite the tremendous amount of love you have for your child, a lot of women come to a point in their life where they start to feel like something is missing. When a woman stops pursuing her own interests, outside of her child, she can find herself lost.

Rest assured that this isn't a working mom versus stay-at-home mom thing, either. But it may take more of an effort for a stay-at-home mother to keep something going for herself outside of her role as Mom. And it is usually when we lock ourselves into a role—any role—that we begin to feel stagnated and stop feeling our own true self.

When we feed our creative energy in some way—even if it is ever so slightly—that creative energy can build upon itself. Feeding your self opens up new and dormant parts of you. And this process feeds upon itself, too. The more space you allow yourself to open up for yourself, the less stuck you will begin to feel.

## Ask yourself:

*When was the last time I did something that* was just *for me?*

*What were the things that used to inspire me? How has that changed?*

*What can I imagine fitting back into my life—even if it's just for twenty minutes a day?*

*What have I always wanted to learn about that I never had the chance to? What is stopping me now?*

*What does it mean to be a Mom? Who was my role model, both now and in the past? How much do I want to be like that person, and how do I want to be different?*

*Am I truly living out my way of being a mother, or am I just following someone else's way?*

A lot of my clients feel guilty about the idea of making more time for their own self. It's like there is some sort of unwritten rule that a wife and mother who creates time for herself is somehow shameful.

My response is this: Think about how much you give to your child now. Now imagine if there was more of you to give.

The more you take care of yourself, the more you can take care of another person. And the more you give to yourself, the more you have to give to someone else. Including your child.

If your cup is full, you'll only be able to give what you absolutely need to—and there will probably be some resentment. But what if you could make some space in your cup to fill it with what inspires you?

A good way to look at all this is to think of a time when you were feeling very alive, and you felt the vital energy within you. Now imagine the people who were around you at that time. How was your energy affecting them? The point is that when you replenish your cup, you can give more qualitatively to others, including your kids.

Any time you feel stuck, there is an opportunity to re-find yourself. And the journey can be fulfilling—as long as you have an open heart, let go of guilt, and focus on being true to yourself.

Whether you just got pregnant, just had a baby, just sent your child to his first day of school, or just started your life as an empty-nester, seize the opportunity to give yourself the space you need.

*Dr. Niloo Dardashti is a psychologist and coach in NYC. She has authored two books,* Into the Twilight Haze*, and* Fifty Shades of Women's Desires. *Dr. Dardashti also trains other professionals in holistic mental health treatment. In 2011, Dr. Dardashti created a documentary that takes a deeper look at the pop culture phenomenon of* Twilight. *The film explores common issues that many* *couples face, in addition to explaining some of the cross-generational fascination with the* Twilight *phenomena.*

---

### Selene's Story

*I've realized that there is a different meaning to this step of accepting people for who they are. We must accept that they want different things than we do—or what we want for them. To try and force them to do what we "advise" hurts both of us. This is, of course, true for parents. The hardest thing I've found (out of the many hard things) about parenting is to not try to influence my sons to follow paths I cleared for them. They get to choose which path to go down—and that can be heartbreaking! But we must remember that the love is still there, and it will flourish when we act unselfishly.*

---

This side of accepting people for who they are is aptly represented in the following Zen proverb:

### *"Let go or be dragged."*

I envision this as someone grabbing hold of a rear bumper as a car speeds away.

I could see myself clinging to a bumper. Okay—I *have* clung to a bumper. (Metaphorically.)

When I realized that my sons were on their own paths, and they didn't really need me anymore, I lost it. It was just as bad as a boyfriend breaking up with me. Worse—because I had, after all, invested my heart and life into these boys for so many years. And what did I have left? What would I do with myself, all alone?

It's fear—blind panic—which makes us cling. We must summon the strength to let love conquer that terror.

Because, after all, the job of parents is to raise our children so that they can effectively function in the world. It's like we're long-term surrogates.

Our kids will always love us, and we can talk with them and visit them, but we cannot continue to make them the center of our lives. We must center our own lives. This book, hopefully, is giving you ideas and practical ways to forge your new life.

This also applies to anyone who is moving in a different direction than you—a sibling, a friend, you name it. People change, and not at the same rate. Wish them well. Let them go.

Don't get dragged.

---

## A NOTE FROM THE EXPERT: SCOTT WEISNER, JD, PSYD

Here are nine simple steps to increase the happiness that you experience as a parent by decreasing the stress parenting causes (although they are all connected):

1. *Decrease the amount of responsibilities on your plate.* Many parents work, are active members of the PTA, have multiple after-school activities for their children, and then have to manage the household responsibilities. After all of this, then they agree to work the bake sale at their local church or collect cans for the local Toys For Tots program. If you can place healthy limits on the number of tasks you take on for both you and your child, life can be simpler, with less responsibilities, less pressure, and more time for pleasurable moments with your child.

2. *Choose your battles: Kids will be kids.* They will be silly when you need them to be serious, have difficulty sitting still, make inappropriate jokes, horseplay with their siblings, touch what they should not be touching, and stay awake when they are exhausted and need sleep. If you choose to criticize, yell, or punish a child for every little infraction, neither you nor your child will be happy with the time you spend with each other. Set up a system where you can have your child recognize there are going to be serious times when more is expected of them and times where they will get an extra warning. During the serious times, the battle is on, but when it is the weekend and everyone is in their pajamas, decide if you need to be so rigid or if you can let it slide to keep the nice day going.

3. *Know you and your child's current level of frustration tolerance.* If you have no patience or tolerance for frustration, you are more likely to get frustrated with your child. That frustration turns a pleasant time into an unhappy experience for both you and your children. Any adult who is stressed has a tendency to be more critical and more punitive. Similarly, any child who is already in a negative place is going to give their parent a harder time. By keeping an eye on both your and your child's level of frustration, you can decide if it is better to address an issue later with a moody child or let your partner handle the kids for a little bit if you have less patience than normal.

4. *Give yourself a break.* No parent can do everything—especially if they are overstressed. You need to be able to take a step back and do something to relieve some of their stress. This may involve taking a hot shower to relax, indulging in a piece of chocolate cake, listening to a favorite song (or two), or having a glass of wine. Taking a few minutes to reduce your stress level can make your interactions with your children more pleasant. When our kids see us in a good mood, it is contagious.

5. *Be consistent.* Children who have consistency in their lives tend to do better in school and have less mental health issues as adults. Giving your child the gift of consistency not only gives them an advantage, but it also makes for a healthier relationship with your

child. Imagine if at work your boss constantly changed his expectations of what he wanted from your performance. One week he wanted you to complete something one way, and then the next week he wanted you to complete it another way. It would drive most people mad. Imagine how a child would feel if a parent keeps changing the rules on them. When a child has a clear understanding of the rules and knows the rules are consistently enforced, they are less likely to challenge them and more likely to accept consequences for their mistakes. In addition, consistency allows them to feel safe and learn that their world is a predictable place. When children experience this, they are happier, and their relationship with you as their parent is more secure and more pleasurable.

6. *Avoid parenting decisions made out of anger or escalating.* A parent that is unpredictable and angry escalates the situation. It is impossible to get pleasure out of parenting if you are unable to spend time laughing, joking, playing, or pleasantly interacting with your child because they are avoiding you.

7. *Show an interest in their interests.* We choose to be friends with people with whom we share common interests. However, with our children, it is a crapshoot. If we want to maintain a relationship, we need to be able to meet them on their level and show them that we are interested in their interests and that we want to both spend time with them and share the pleasure that they get out of the things they like.

8. *You can never give enough compliments.* Studies show that people are more sensitive to negative feedback. With children, most will tell you that their parents are always on top of them, telling them they did this wrong or that wrong. Therefore, make sure you pour on the compliments to try to balance out all the correcting you have to do.

9. *Make sure to repair when you make a mistake.* It is hard to have a relationship with someone that does not repair mistakes. So, in the (obviously ridiculously rare) moments a parent makes a mistake—like accusing the wrong child of making a mess or starting a fight—it is important to be able to apologize and repair the relationship.

*Dr. Scott Weisner, JD, has a Masters in forensic psychology from John Jay College of Criminal Justice, a Juris Doctorate from Tulane Law School, and a Doctorate in psychology from Long Island University. Weisner has practiced psychology for the past fifteen years, conducting individual, group, and family therapy. He also performs psychological evaluations and testifies as an expert witness. He currently works for a state psychiatric hospital and has a private practice working with adults, adolescents, and children.*

## Bosses

Our bosses are also human, whether it seems that way or not. They have feelings and have likely been through the wringer like you. Perhaps they're using their power to make up for their lack of it in their personal lives. Or… who knows? You're not their therapist, so don't waste your time thinking about them. Once you leave the workplace for the day, it's time to let them go and take care of yourself.

During the day, I would employ empathy toward them and focus on getting the job done.

If you can't tolerate them, perhaps you should leave. No matter how wonderful a job should be in theory, if it's not good in practice, find another one.

*"People take different roads seeking fulfillment and happiness. Just because they're not on your road doesn't mean they've gotten lost."*

—Dalai Lama XIV

---

## Concrete Action

# Acceptance

1. Write about a person you are having difficulty with in your gratitude journal, or write a poem about them.

2. Think about literature you've read. Reflect on characters' relationships and how issues were or weren't resolved. What would you do in those situations? Write notes and compare to your real-life relationships.

3. Write a card or letter to a person you've had difficulty with, thanking them for their unique gifts or just acknowledging that you care. If the person has passed away, you might bring it to their resting place, or have a ceremony where you read it aloud to them.

4. Change your mindset toward the person with whom you are having difficulty. Do not allow any negative feelings toward them. Instead, think only kind and accepting thoughts. Do not badmouth them or complain about them. Try not to think about them at all when you are not in their presence—but if you do, be positive and forgiving. Focus on any good qualities they possess, and/or practice empathizing with them.

5. If you can avoid a situation where you will encounter a person you have difficulty with, do it. If you must see them, keep the meeting as short as possible. Be positive, kind, and forgiving.

6. End any relationships that don't work for you, if at all possible. This doesn't have to be dramatic. You don't need to declare: "I'm done with you!" This just begets more negativity. Keep away from them! Quietly disengage. (More about this in our next step.)

# RID YOURSELF OF WHAT YOU NO LONGER NEED

T hink of everything we cover in this step as simplifying your life— clearing your mind and your path to happy.

I spent my earlier years weighing myself down with complexities, only to recognize my need for simplicity when I was in my forties.

This is a huge step, because it covers both outer and inner turmoil. Yes, the proper description for anything you no longer need is "turmoil" because it creates chaos inside us. Think of it in terms of weather. Some of it is a black cloud over us, some of it is rain, and some is an out-and-out whirling tornado.

All of it is contrary to happy.

What I'm referring to is people, habits/belief systems, and tangible objects (clutter). We'll tackle each of these on its own, but in the end I think you'll find stark correlations between them, and you may very well have been circling them all without even realizing it. It's funny—though not really—how the clutter we keep in our homes causes disharmony, much like our toxic relationships.

It's hard to recognize the toxicity of something you're immersed in. That's why, just as you must detoxify from a physical addiction, you must emotionally detox. Let's get started!

*"I'm sorry, Mama. I'm cleaning out my closet."*

—Eminem

I love this line, because—like many of Eminem's lyrics—it works on more than one level. Eminem had a famously bad childhood, and he channeled his rage into rapping. But he could not bear to carry all of the emotional baggage of his childhood. This lyric is metaphorical—he's clearing out all of the horror, pain, and dysfunction in the closet of his mind—but the image is concrete and could absolutely be applied literally. And the master touch is the apology to his mother. Because when we move on, the hardest part is often the guilt. Are we leaving people behind, still in their old patterns? What if they need us? They often do need us, but only to play the role opposite them and generate the drama and conflict they're used to. You're used to it, too! You might feel a tremendous pull toward them; you may feel a staggering guilt and/or loss at leaving them. And these people will tug at you, crying, screaming, begging, threatening… using any tactic to keep you in your pattern with them. You must be strong. You are not their keeper; you are not letting them down. Your obligation is to yourself. You deserve to be happy, and these relationships are roadblocks to that goal.

I'm sure you have people in your life who don't create out-and-out drama, but they bring you down with a constant sob story or negative attitude. You don't have to make a declaration that you're done with them. What I'm suggesting is that you create boundaries with them.

## What the heck are boundaries?

Sure, you know what the word "boundary" means—but do you know how to apply boundaries to your life?

To apply boundaries to your life, you must take a stand—not allowing people to act in a manner that makes you uncomfortable, demeans you, offends you, or in any way deprives you of even a moment of the happy life you deserve.

This sounds hard! And at first, it is. It's terrifying, because the little kid inside of you who wants to be loved is screaming to do anything to keep people.

But if someone treats you badly, that's not love.

The clock is ticking! What if you knew how many hours of life you were allotted, and could schedule allotments? Would you hand over "x" amount of hours to someone else, to use at their discretion without any consideration of you? Guess what, that's exactly what you're doing—except you don't know the percentage of hours you've sacrificed until you die. David Cassidy's last words were reportedly, "So much wasted time." Don't waste your time on people who don't deserve it.

My Aunt Olga used to call them "gimmes" because they were all about what you could give them. She also called such a person "a bag with a hole in it." You just keep filling and filling, and whatever you've put in comes out the other end. Is this your idea of a productive use of your precious time?

I didn't understand how to apply boundaries in my life until I was in my thirties.

I was so desperate for companionship and what I interpreted as love that I would put up with any bad behavior and not speak up for myself. It was a vicious circle: I had low self-esteem, and my actions re-affirmed it. I was proving to myself that my belief system was right—I was worthless. But once I started setting boundaries—from the simple yet powerful act of saying "no" to dismissing toxic people from my presence—my self-esteem rose, and a new circle began. My healthy boundaries removed toxic people from my life (maybe not literally, but they faded to the rear when they lost their power over me, and it was like they were gone because they ceased to matter). And I realized that I was worthy—of good relationships, of success, of happiness. All these things go hand in hand.

And the more my self-esteem rose, the easier it was to create—and uphold—boundaries.

In the beginning it will be tough! People will do anything to keep you in line, playing the role you always have—to keep the drama going. Drama is chaos, and it is just about impossible to find happy in chaos. Happy dwells with peace.

You will also repel new toxic people, because your boundaries will be so clear that they can be sensed without words. You will build an iron aura around you that toxicity cannot penetrate. After a while, it won't even try.

## Concrete Action

# Remove toxicity

1. Each morning, step outside and take a deep breath in. When you let it out, think of how grateful you are for this day. Take another deep breath in. When you release it, think about the toxic people you know all in a little boat, drifting down a river, far away from you.

2. Say no to anything you don't want to do! It gets easier and easier. (Obviously, I don't mean work, lessons, or anything you're legally obligated to do! I'm referring to requests, invitations, and offers.)

3. Don't engage. It takes two to tango, and you don't have to dance. My ex-husband used to say seemingly innocuous things that would trigger me into prior experiences, and suddenly I'd be Sharon Stone flipping out in *Casino*. Don't let this be you. You have control over your emotions!

4. If this is a big issue for you, consider joining Al-Anon, which is for family members of alcoholics. A toxic person exhibits the same traits as an alcoholic, without necessarily being one. I joined Al-Anon and stayed in for about a year, and it was there that I learned about building boundaries. I also learned to stop trying to reach "unreachable" people. My favorite thing I heard someone say in Al-Anon is, "Trying to talk to some people is like talking to an eggplant. Does an eggplant listen to you? Does it respond to you? Are you able to relate to it in any way? Try envisioning these impossible people as eggplants." This analogy did the trick for me! Al-Anon has books to read and slogans. They can be comforting, but also, possibly, annoying. I didn't like the slogans because they're all clichés—and I'm a writer! But I appreciated the sentiment, and I did use the books for a while. I advise you to do what they suggest: "Take what you want, and leave the rest."

# Habits

*"We are what we repeatedly do."*

—Will Durant's interpretation of Aristotle

We often develop habits designed to protect us from perceived dangers, unpleasantness, and pain. Many times these are rooted in childhood, when we were learning about the world and conceived things a certain way. You're not a child anymore, and the things you continue to do may now be hurting you.

A habit may be to spend lunch reading by yourself, instead of joining a group of co-workers. When you were a kid, perhaps you didn't think you fit in with others, so you found a spot in the corner and holed up with The Hardy Boys (okay, that's what I did). But as it turns out, the other kids really did want to be your friends, something I learned years later by reconnecting with other kids from my elementary school on Facebook. You can't go back in time and change your lunchroom choices—but you can make some changes now. Maybe there are some people at work who would love to chat with you!

This is just an example, based on my own experiences. I perceived myself to be an outsider and built up defensive habits to "protect" myself. But we need companionship and friendship! We crave connection. Whatever your habits are, take a close look at them, and consider whether they're serving your current best interests. You might be surprised at the answer.

# FROM THE DOCTOR'S DESK: LINDSAY S. WEISNER, PSY.D

Sometimes feeling happy really is as simple as listening to your body's cues.

Mental health professionals have long used the acronym HALT (Hungry, Angry, Lonely, Tired) to help recovering addicts avoid relapse. Why? Well, no big surprise, there is a huge connection between the mind and the body—and vice versa. Physical sensations like hunger and lack of sleep can trigger emotions that we can misread as anxiety or depression. Feeling angry or lonely can make you feel like you have a physical need for something—usually something not so good for you, like drugs or alcohol. Or something more benign, like carbs, greasy food, or that emotionally-unavailable guy that you just can't seem to shake. And if you think giving in to a need that is motivated by anger or loneliness helps your situation—you're wrong.

Next time you feel sad or anxious and you can't figure out why, go back to the basics and think HALT. Am I hungry? Angry? Lonely? Tired? If you can identify the problem, you can fix it before your emotions start spiraling out of control. Eat something. Drink some extra water. Call a friend and vent. Make plans with someone you love. Make sure you're taking care of yourself.

## Concrete Action

# Breaking bad habits

1.  Acknowledge the habit. We tend to push things we don't want to deal with into the back of our minds. To break a habit you first have to admit its existence to yourself.

2.  Write about it in your notebook. How long have you had this habit? How did it begin? What purpose does it serve you? List the pros and cons of this habit. (Yes, bad habits can have "pros"—which is part of the reason you engage in them.) You can also keep a log about the habit, over days or weeks.

3.  Make a decision to break this habit. There's no rush—you can do this at your own speed. Once you've made this commitment to yourself, every time you find yourself thinking about engaging in the habit, distract your thoughts with something else. Yes, you need to play a head game with yourself. You can also give yourself a reward for not engaging in the habit. (See Step Eight for reward ideas.)

4.  Try meditation. It has been credited for breaking many habits!

5.  You may want support, like a group or a therapist. There's no shame in this!

6.  For particularly tough, self-destructive habits, you may need to address your belief system behind them.

## Beliefs

*"There is nothing good or bad, but thinking makes it so."*

—William Shakespeare,
*Hamlet*

We are often our own worst enemy. Our belief systems can bring us down, because how we see the world is what the world presents to us. It is not easy to change our belief system. We must consciously work at reprogramming ourselves.

It's easy to say you're going to let go of a belief, but you have to really believe that you've let go of it. This takes much dedication and concentration. You established these beliefs for a reason—something convinced you that the world operates in a certain manner, or that you are a certain thing in relation to the world. Honor the past, and then move forward. Don't beat yourself up for whatever the you of the past believed and manifested—there was a reason for it. But that reason is over. You are not the person you were, and your belief system must change to reflect that new you! (Or, the "you" you want and deserve to be! The HAPPY you!)

This sounds so difficult, but I assure you, it gets easier and easier as you apply it.

An example of this is to change the belief that you are not loveable, or that you are not worthy of a loving relationship. This may stem from a childhood trauma like divorce or abandonment. Or, it might have been an offhanded comment someone told you when you were young, and you literally took it to heart. In any case, you must now teach your subconscious this new belief. Or you doom yourself to relationships that manifest your belief that you're unworthy.

We all want something more. Something better. We all have dreams and desire and purpose and passions and then—we stop ourselves.

We stop ourselves with doubt, or derailment—by ourselves or by others, or by something that we label "practical," but that is really "sacrificial."

We stop ourselves because we are afraid.

We stop ourselves because we feel guilt or shame.

Isn't it time to take back the power, the control we have handed over to emotions of insecurity?

---

## A NOTE FROM THE EXPERT: DR. NILOO DARDASHTI

Using Hollywood's representation of "love" as an example for how things should be in life—and in a relationship—is an inevitable set-up for disappointment.

In case you haven't noticed, there is a clear formula to love stories as they are expressed through film, and the story almost always involves some sort of unrequited love that becomes requited by the end of the film. So the film ends where the real relationship actually begins.

But, what happens *after* the obstacles are removed and the reality of routine life kick in? What happens after Edward and Bella finally get married at the end of the Twilight books? Is the life, and relationship, as exciting?

As you may be guessing, probably not.

Romance novels and chick flicks are generally based on the beginning stages of a relationship—when dopamine is at an all-time high and euphoria is the chief feeling between partners. In fact, most films about couples that have been married for a few years represent the characters as bored and unfulfilled.

Usually the obstacle, or staleness, in these stories involves an affair. And an affair also involves the novel, beginning stage feelings between feelings.

The obstacle of an affair serves to bring the couple closer in some ways. But most people, in most relationships, don't experience the same dramatic experiences that we see in the theater. Working things out takes time, and sometimes couples therapy, and a lot of work, and a lot of willingness to do the work.

This all happens gradually and results in subtle changes over time.

So let's face it: Hollywood reinforces the illusion of another person "completing" us. And it is not uncommon to read novels or watch movies and find yourself crossing the line from enjoying a fantasy world to falling into a delusion of what your own relationship *should* be like.

We all seek connectedness and chemistry in our relationships. We all want to feel the passion and attunement that we see people enjoying on the big screen. But it can be dangerous when we use the fantasy on the screen as a focus of comparison for our reality-based relationships.

I had a patient in her mid-twenties, Jenna, who used to compare her real-life relationships to a film in which the leading male character made a grand gesture to win back his girlfriend. Jenna had been thinking about breaking up with her boyfriend and reported that the only way she would know if her boyfriend was truly committed to her was if he performed some grand gesture for her, the same way the male actor in the film had done for his girlfriend.

It took some time in therapy for Jenna to be able to see her boyfriend as a whole person himself, rather than a man who was similar to this character in the movie.

I soon learned in a couples session that her boyfriend was, in fact, soft-spoken, and rather unlikely to communicate his feelings through any grand gestures. Jenna's boyfriend felt chronically invalidated and criticized by Jenna for not fitting the ideal image that she held for him. Once Jenna was able to take responsibility for her role in their dynamics, and both parties felt like they were able to be heard in the relationship, their relationship improved.

Maybe it's time to ditch your beliefs about what your relationship *should* be like.

Think this applies to you and your relationship?

Have you ever found yourself comparing your relationship to one in a movie? If so, think back to the film. Did it show what the relationship really looked like once the boy got the girl?

It is okay to have thoughts and ideas about what kind of relationship you want to have when you watch a movie. Maybe you see a relationship you want to emulate. But be careful how much you focus on the good qualities of the idealized other, rather than the possible flaws?

Do you compare your relationship to other couples you know? And how well do you really know them? I bet you don't have any idea what goes on behind closed doors.

*Dr. Niloo Dardashti is a psychologist and coach in NYC. She has authored two books,* Into the Twilight Haze, *and* Fifty Shades of Women's Desires. *Dr. Dardashti also trains other professionals in holistic mental health treatment. In 2011, Dr. Dardashti created a documentary that takes a deeper look at the pop culture phenomenon of* Twilight. *The film explores common issues that many couples face, in addition to explaining some of the cross-generational fascination with the* Twilight *phenomena.*

---

# Doubt

*"Our doubts are traitors, and make us lose the good we oft might win, by fearing to attempt."*

—William Shakespeare, Measure For Measure

Doubt is deadly, because it smothers many dreams. Like a pillow over your face, it silently suffocates.

How did you come to doubt yourself? When you were a kid you knew what you wanted to do—and you believed without question that you would do it.

The answer is usually that someone, or "someones," planted that doubt in you. They may have said, "You're not smart enough" or "You're not talented enough." They may have said, "Hardly anyone makes it in that business, why would you?" They may have made fun of you for your ambition. No matter how they phrased it, the message was the same: "Quit dreaming."

So, you did.

---

### Selene's Story

Both of my sons danced and really loved it. Unfortunately, on Long Island it's not the norm for boys to dance. They both stopped, even though they were quite good and clearly enjoyed themselves. I really think they wanted to be like everyone else. They started to care what people thought. I wish I could've supported them more and found a way to persuade them to continue, because it was great seeing them perform so passionately.

*"Doubt kills more dreams than failure ever will."*

—Suzy Kassem

## Derailment

You found out you could make a lot of money being an investment banker. So, even though you knew you were meant to be a pastry chef, you headed off to business school and then Wall Street. Too bad you never believed the old saying, "Money can't buy you happiness."

Or you learned that there are easier ways to make a living than your passion. It would take so long to fulfill your passion! It would be so hard! Why go to all that trouble?

*"Talent is cheaper than table salt. What separates the talented individual from the successful one is a lot of hard work."*

—Stephen King

Bottom line: Has an easy or lucrative (in money alone) career fulfilled you? What would happen if you took a risk and tried to follow your passion, rather than your fears?

---

## A NOTE FROM THE EXPERT: DAVID MAHLER

For my fortieth birthday, my wife had a big surprise in store for me. She secretly arranged a trip to Las Vegas with my three college friends from U.C. Berkeley. The four of us had not been alone as a group for nearly twenty years. I was totally unaware of the trip until a few days before. My wife arranged for a limo to pick us up at the Las Vegas airport and take us to the Aria Resort & Casino where she had booked two fantastic suites. She even arranged for a bottle of Scotch to be waiting when we got there.

It didn't take long before we fell right back into our old ways—telling cheesy jokes, laughing at anything and everything, and mostly just reminiscing. We told stories of silly adventures we'd had in college, like the times in the middle of the night that we'd sneak into the extensive network of steam tunnels underneath U.C. Berkeley to explore, or "spelunking," as we liked to call it. We had so many stories that had faded over time but were refreshed and renewed just by being together.

During that trip, my friend Jay and I talked about working on a project together. We had both been interested in starting a business, and for the first time in our lives, it seemed everything could line up right for this dream to be made into a reality.

When the trip was finished, the idea of starting a business stuck in the back of my mind. A few weeks later, Jay and I followed up on our conversation. We tossed around a few random ideas in a brainstorming session, but in the end only one thing stood out: The best part of seeing one another after so long was retelling all those old stories from college.

Everyone has stories from their lives. They don't have to be grand adventures of fame and fortune to be interesting. Just everyday stories you might tell friends over a few drinks.

Stories give you insight into others lives. Stories also teach you about yourself; you get to cognitively go through an experience, without having actually ever been there.

We were, of course, aware of NPR's "The Moth," where folks tell stories on stage in front of a live audience. But these stories have been curated, edited, condensed, and rehearsed. We wanted something different. We wanted to create an open community online where everyone could tell their story, raw and unedited.

Throughout my life, I've had tons of ideas pop in my head about businesses or side projects. However, a combination of bad timing and my own doubts and fears always got in the way.

This time, however, was different. First, the timing was right for both of us. Our kids were not babies anymore; we were comfortable with our jobs and no longer trying to "climb the ladder."

The biggest difference this time was that when my usual doubts and fears popped up, I was ready. I viewed these doubts and fears as potential problems that could arise. All I had to do was come up with potential solutions.

### *"I don't have time."*

How could I possibly find the time to start a new business and website? I have a wife and young children. I have a challenging, full-time job, and my priorities are clear: family first, work second, the rest is negotiable.

I have learned to examine carefully where my time goes every day and how much that matches what I want out of life. For me, this means some "sacrifices." Most of the time, upon further examination, it turns out that these are not true "sacrifices" at all.

I don't really need to catch up with the news every day. In fact, since when does following the news ever bring me happiness?

And do I really need to watch every single episode of *The Office*? Again?

Sure, it is enjoyable, but at some point, I just feel bad that I didn't do something else with all that time.

What is the monetary value of my time worth so that I can have the extra time to spend on following my passion? Can I afford a house cleaning service every now and then so that I can make some progress on other goals? Or perhaps if that costs too much, I can just accept the house being a little dirtier.

Finding time for my passions has also meant finding ways to be more efficient in my life. At work, I will sometimes spend time waffling between two choices just to make a decision that was my first instinct, anyway. I learned to trust myself and to be more decisive.

### *"This new project would be too complex."*

When you are standing at the beginning and trying to comprehend the end, it is a lot to handle. It can feel too complicated and too overwhelming, and it would be so much easier to just stop before you even start.

For my business, we needed to pick a domain name, start an LLC, figure out what kind of legal requirements we would have to follow, and how did we even figure out where to host the site? Should we have a book? A podcast? The list goes on and on!

So Jay and I broke up everything into smaller, easier steps.

Task A: Research LLCs and alternatives.

Task B: Choose between the options from Task A.

Task C: Get a PO box for a business address.

Now we were dealing with truly actionable items. When looking at those singular smaller tasks, my mind changed from, "this is not possible" to "I can totally do that!" I didn't let myself get overwhelmed by the rest of the project, I concentrated and focused in like a laser on the subset. We moved the ball forward week by week, small task by small task.

Completing subtasks feels great. And it's important to keep in mind that the whole, huge project doesn't have to be done overnight. You can take as long as you want.

Even if it takes a year or more to get to our destination with the business, the time will pass regardless. At the end of that time, do I want to be the owner of a new business, or do I want to be an armchair expert on *The Office*?

For me, it is undoubtedly the former.

### *"I'm not qualified."*

Sometimes, beyond complexity and time constraints, we let self-doubt get in the way.

Who do I think I am to be starting a website and business around sharing personal stories? I'm not a website developer, I don't have an MBA, and English wasn't even my strong subject in school.

After twenty years of working in a challenging, complex area of cloud computing (essentially, working on thousands of computers that run in a massive central facility instead of running in your home or office), I have learned that a lot more people are "winging it" than you would expect. Even amongst "experts" on a topic, there is a lot of looking things up on Google, last-minute cramming, and moving forward without total understanding.

Early in my engineering career, I was faced with a new topic of engineering that seemed far too complicated for my mind to grasp. I didn't even know how to broach it. I asked a more experienced engineer how he could possibly feel confident enough to approach the problem. His answer was so simple and yet so enlightening to me. "We are smart enough guys, if a bunch of other people figured out, why can't we figure it out too?"

This has now become my philosophy with objectives that feel over my head or that I feel "not qualified" to embark on. Sure, I've never build a website before, and I've never started a business before. Yet, millions of people have done just that; there isn't something that makes all of them more qualified or "special" than me. They all did it, and I certainly can too!

I can find the time, I can deconstruct the complexity and make it approachable, and I can make myself more qualified.

### *"What will they think?"*

In my past, I have had this artificial fear of embarrassing myself. What will they think when I tell them I'm starting a website? Will they think it's ridiculous? Will they mock me behind my back?

It turns out that most people have responded really positively when I tell them what I am doing. I would like to think that is in part because we all have hopes, dreams, and endeavors that we are trying to work up the courage to try.

And if someone is bringing a negative energy and vibe to something that makes me happy, it's possible that I need to develop stronger boundaries with that person. This is for me and my happiness, not for anyone else.

### *"I might fail."*

So what?

Many successful entrepreneurs have failed plenty of times before finding success. My life will change no matter where this business goes, in that I will experience a new first in my life. Plus, I have reconnected with an old friend, my co-founder. I have also been able to learn quite a lot about business—without having to pay for my MBA. I have had the opportunity to read some fantastic stories submitted to the site and to learn about topics I would never have sought out on my own.

And when all is said and done, I will have the immense satisfaction of knowing that I tried, and I didn't let my fears hold me back.

*David Mahler lives in California with his beloved wife, Erin, and their two sons, Ronan and Sean. David started his career as a technical trainer and then continued as an engineer at IBM, Cisco, Hewlett-Packard, and Myspace (remember Myspace?). In the last few years Dave has stepped outside his comfort zone by creating his own YouTube Channel and beginning piano lessons at the age of forty. Dave is the co-founder of The Story Pub at https://thestorypub.com, which launched in February 2019.*

# Fear

You may think that fear is just like doubt, but it's a special kind of sinister. Doubt is a thick fog we can muster up the courage to plod through. Fear is a wall we hit in our path. We must find a way to scale it or knock it down. This often feels impossible, and we collapse to the ground.

The crazy thing? We built that wall ourselves. Once we realize that, we can find our way past it.

*"The only thing we have to fear is fear itself."*

—Franklin D. Roosevelt

# Shame

*"The mistake ninety-nine percent of humanity made… was being ashamed of what they were…"*

—J.K. Rowling

There are so many reasons we feel shame and many we can't even remember. Something happens to us in a moment, and we are scarred. It can be something we see, hear, or endue. It can be a misinterpretation, or it can be a devastating truth we were unequipped to handle.

### Selene's Story

 When I was little, I knew I was a writer. I knew before I'd even learned what a writer was. The moment I held a pencil, I knew that I was meant to use it. It was my tool.

This calmed me and warmed my heart. It was my assurance of my place in the world.

As time went on, I learned about writing and began to do it. I wrote stories and poems. More, more, more! When I wasn't writing, I was reading.

I remember well the time that inspiration struck in Arthur Treacher's Fish & Chips restaurant. I was with my mom and my aunt. I wrote everything on napkins—for a long time! They were patient and didn't force me to leave.

That was the beginning of a mystery I was writing. Undaunted, I wrote and revised for years. I went to NYU and majored in English, which exposed me to a lot of literature, but there wasn't much on the writing side. So I took a writing night class at a local community college and then joined the teacher's writing group. I even met a successful author who critiqued my work and gave me a million suggestions. (Maybe not a million, but it felt like it. Some people would have been discouraged by the amount of work I needed to do, but I was ignited because someone had shown me the way.)

But everything came to a halt one day, when I put a voice-activated tape recorder under my bed. I suspected that my live-in boyfriend was cheating on me with a friend of ours. I not only heard the upsetting confirmation, but I also heard them making fun of my writing efforts. They were laughing at me—mocking me! This was a double betrayal, and at that vulnerable point in my life, it devastated me. I stopped writing.

*Literally just stopped. I threw down my pencil and gave up.*

*Incidentally, not only did these people have no authority on writing—neither had ever read a word I'd written. They were making fun of my exuberance and unwavering belief that I would make it as a writer. The truth is, they were jealous because they had no such pursuit. He worked at a cigarette wholesaler and she worked as a secretary. When he got laid off, she quit her job and they did drugs together all day (as well as other things, apparently.) These were not ambitious people. To make themselves feel better, they ridiculed me.*

*I let their remarks end my dreams. For ten years I didn't write. I opened up a gift basket store, pouring my creativity into baskets—and I was obsessively good at them. I was always designing them and looking for cool stuff to put in them. I stayed late into the night restocking and setting up beautiful displays.*

*The only writing I did was for advertisements. The best time was Easter, when I could add in a few word puns: "An eggciting sale!" "An eggstravaganza!" "You'll find eggcellent baskets here!" You get the eggxact idea.*

*I got married and had two sons. And it was those sons who changed everything.*

*A parent worries about their mortality. What if something happens to me? I wondered. How will my sons know that I loved them?*

*Writing sprang to my mind. To me, words were love. I would express my love to my boys by writing a book and dedicating it to them—and they would always have it!*

*This was an awakening from hibernation.*

*Once I allowed myself to think about writing again, I was reborn. It was a second chance, a reprieve—I was a fish released from the hook and tossed back into the sea. I swam and swam, glorious… reveling!*

*I appreciated my writing so much… and I still do.*

*I was lucky… or else my passion was so strong that it refused to stay buried forever. Or maybe both. In any case, I know what it's like to walk around without my true purpose, trying to fill that huge hole in my heart with something, anything! Creating the gift basket business was a great distraction, but luckily for me I didn't wind up making baskets for the rest of my life. That wasn't my passion, and I did feel the difference unconsciously. I just tried my hardest to ignore it, because I didn't feel like I deserved it.*

*Aha! Now we come to a deep-seated reason why people don't pursue what they love.*

*They feel like they don't deserve it.*

*Some feel ashamed of themselves—but they don't even know why. My shame was the real reason why I allowed that conversation between my boyfriend and my friend to destroy my dreams.*

*I let them destroy my dreams.*

*I didn't even realize I was giving my consent. That's the insidious part.*

*If you identify with this, please seek help. Although this book will set you on your path toward finding happy, you might need personal attention to dig out that deep-rooted shame, once and for all. Because if you don't get out the whole root, it will just manifest again—a destructive weed spreading, ravaging your beautiful garden. (This is the problem with weeds—not that they exist, but that they overpower and suppress every other growing thing. Think about this happening inside you.)*

# A NOTE FROM THE EXPERT: DR. MAGGIE

For the average person, the words guilt and shame are used interchangeably, and often without much distinction. But for the clinician, there is a world of difference.

You know the expression, *It's like bringing a knife to a gun fight*?

The knife is the guilt. But the gun is your shame. It's the gun that delivers the bigger punch to your heart/ego/self-image.

If this strikes you as an odd or ill-fitting analogy, I can assure you that this analogy comes from personal experience. Over the last fifteen years, I have survived both the universe of guilt and the stratosphere of shame.

So, what is guilt? Guilt is how you feel in relation to the other people in your life; guilt is that interactive experience that occurs when your actions or inactions impact others. Did you forget to call your best friend on her birthday? Cheat on a test? Or perhaps you mistakenly tipped the waitress less than you "should" have.

You feel guilty when you believe that you have wronged someone. The tricky part here is that one person's definition of the word "wrong" is based on society's standards. Guilt makes no difference what you, yourself, believe is just or right.

You can feel guilty for something you have done regardless of what your intention actually was. This awful feeling of self-blame or failure can arise regardless of if your (perceived) action was accidental or unconscious. For example, you might feel badly a classmate tripped over your backpack.

Guilt can also arise regardless of if your (perceived) action was imagined, like if you think something you said hurt your friend's feelings.

This awful feeling of self-blame or failure can be paralyzing, pervasive, crippling, and most of all, and in the least, incredibly uncomfortable. The problem with guilt is that when you compare yourself to others or to society's norms as a whole, surprisingly, guilt is not a very powerful motivator of change.

Why not? There are two reasons that guilt doesn't help us change our behavior.

First, humans are smart creatures, and we are pretty good at making ourselves feel better in the short-term by latching on to so-called "thinking errors."

Feeling guilty for cheating on that test? "It's not so bad, everyone does it."

Upset that your classmate tripped over your stuff? "He is so clumsy, he really should have looked where he was walking."

Worried that your words upset your friend? "Suzie is so sensitive all the time!"

These thinking errors are defense mechanisms. Their sole purpose is to make us feel better about whatever we feel guilty about. And if we feel better, there really is little reason to change our behavior.

The second reason guilt doesn't usually lead to change is that the power for true change comes from a feeling of self-worth and self-love. True change only happens when you not only feel that you *should* do better, but that you *deserve* to be better. And that you want and deserve to feel different, better, and less weighed down by these negative emotions.

So what about shame? Shame tends to follow guilt, like the little brother that always has to tag along and always seems to make everything so much worse. But can shame motivate change?

Once you start feeling guilty for how you wronged someone else—or how you imagine you wronged someone else—you unconsciously make this one act represent who you are as a person, rather than just feeling badly about this one thing that you did. You quickly go from feeling guilt over one action to the nasty heavy black cloud of shame that expands and diffuses over our entire being.

If you have ever studied another language, you know that many cultures distinguish between permanent and impermanent verbs. In Spanish, the verb *ser* and *estar* both mean "to be." *Ser* is used for permanent situations. *Estar* is used for temporary situations. If you are traveling and someone asks you where you are staying (a hotel, friend's house, or AirBnB), your response would be with the verb *estar*. If you are traveling and someone asks you where you are from, or "of," then it is the permanent verb, *ser*, that is used.

We would use a temporary verb with guilt, and a permanent verb with that which guilt grows into: shame.

It is shame that beats you into feelings of self-loathing, unworthiness, and the heart-breaking belief that you are simply unlovable. Shame is like an unrelenting wave, pouring over you. Shame keeps you on your knees with such force that the idea of getting back up feels like an impossible mission, unworthy and undeserving of any real effort.

The longer you linger in this place of shame, unchecked, the more likely actions or inactions and improprieties that lead to continued guilt and then further crushing shame will happen.

I have been there, crushed by shame, and yet, thankfully, I managed to crawl out of that hole to write this piece.

I lived a double life for many years, both professionally and personally.

My finely-tuned defense mechanism of compartmentalizing came in handy. I put the gray areas of life—the facts and feelings that fell in the middle of what I knew I should and should not do—into a closed box in my brain. Eliminating these messy, mushy grays was remarkably helpful on many fronts. My compartmentalization enabled me to lie, deceive, manipulate, and violate boundaries that I never imagined.

And all the while, I was a successful clinician, friend, wife, mother, sister, and daughter.

No one knew the veil I hid under.

I realize now—and possibly, on some level, I knew it then—that my deception was not an act of malice. I meant my loved ones no harm. None at all. And yet, people got hurt.

Through my own therapy, I was able to realize that this actually came from early childhood emotional deprivation. My unmet needs craved attention and yelled at me to be satisfied. At first, I felt guilt about how I had wronged and deceived the people that counted on me. My guilt, the knife that sliced my conscious in half, eventually led to an overwhelming black cloud of shame, infusing its grasp onto my very being. My shame evolved into a direct assault on my very being, my nature, my worth as a human.

Living with shame is existing in a space where you see light, but don't believe it's meant for you. Where somehow the guilt you feel over your actions is the fuel that you use to believe you need to burn your own house down, not trusting you deserve anyone to help you extinguish it.

This was how I felt for a long time before I somehow realized and became aware of how crippling this was for me, and how I didn't want to feel this anymore. There is little we can do to avoid feeling guilt or shame. But if we become more mindful, self-aware, and compassionate with ourselves, we can mitigate the harm that comes from living in shame, to both ourselves and those around us.

When I finally decided that I was ready to make a change, I began to incorporate two practices into every day: meditation and repeating the blessings of self-love and gratefulness. As corny and trite as this might sound, after a few days I realized that self-awareness and self-love made a tremendous impact in surprisingly subtle ways. For example, instead of the strong hold that shame had on my ways of thinking, the grip seemed to loosen. The thoughts that swirled in my mind were less intensely self-critical, kinder, more forgiving.

I soon began to notice that I didn't want to lie, even about very small things, that transparency was a much closer friend of mine, and I started for feel a fuller range of emotions. Compartmentalization was still there, but fading, and I wasn't falling apart. I was actually feeling more momentary episodes of happy, joy, fun, genuine sadness.

Meditation was a tricky thing. You have to find the meditation that is right for you. It can be using a mantra and repeating it or sitting in mindfulness meditation. What I mean by self-love blessings is similar to loving kindness meditation. Self-love blessings allow us to access the compassion inside us—and it is this compassion that runs in opposition to the impact of shame.

In this type of meditation, you actively wish blessings in the form of love and compassion to yourself, another that you care for, and someone you have difficulty or challenge with in your life.

In the beginning, this sort of thinking may feel mechanical and awkward. However the intention to do it starts off as the most important, and then the work is actually starting to feel more of what you express. Sit tight folks, there is something very real to it.

Gratefulness practice is a huge part of countering the effects of heavy guilt and shame. Especially with shame, you are crushed by the weight of self-loathing and self-blame so much so that being—and feeling—grateful is very far away. Your universe is selfish, small, tight, and cramped with your own internal mess, so to widen your view and look at the world from a different lens feels nonexistent. Now, every morning I practice saying the things I am grateful for out loud. Even if I don't feel grateful in that moment, I say it anyway.

Remember, the practice of these exercises is just that: practice, consistent, gentle, and consistent again. It's like a muscle that needs to be worked out. The muscle of self-compassion that atrophied as a result of guilt and shame. We can't expect the muscle to just become stronger over time and then become grateful for that. We must make it stronger even when it feels weak.

This is hard and takes the motivation to realize you want more, better, and you are willing to work on it, as awkward as it feels, and as much as the shame tries to tell you otherwise. This was true for me, and it can be true for you too.

Sometimes, the unraveling is all we need to make ourselves truly whole again.

*Dr. Maggie\* has spent most of her twenty-year career providing psychological services in hospital and outpatient settings, specializing in anxiety, depression, trauma, and addiction. She has also worked in more corporate settings merging business and psychology and providing mindfulness meditation training. Dr. Maggie specializes in providing intervention to adults who have experienced a variety of life stressors, including burn out, interpersonal and/or work difficulties, and life transitions leading to suffering and disharmony. She can be reached at DrMaggieMindful@gmail.com.*

*\*Not her real name*

*"Don't you think the things people are most ashamed of are things they can't help?"*

—C.S. Lewis, Till We Have Faces

*"No one can make you feel inferior without your consent."*

—Eleanor Roosevelt

---

*"Soul, if you want to learn secrets,*
*your heart must forget about*
*shame and dignity.*
*You are God's lover,*
*yet you worry*
*what people*
*are saying."*

—Rumi

---

## Concrete Action

# Changing your beliefs

1. Just as you needed to acknowledge your bad habit, you must acknowledge that your belief system needs to be adjusted because it no longer suits you.

2. Make a decision to release your old beliefs and replace them with new ones. Write down any feelings you have about this in your notebook, and then, when you're ready, write yourself a letter, contract, or even a poem declaring your commitment to this change.

3. Have a ceremony to commemorate your commitment to change. You can light candles, use sage, drink a tremendous amount of alcohol, and re-read what you wrote in your notebook aloud to the universe.

4. Check out the law of attraction. It's the concept that your thoughts become things, and it has been used with phenomenal results throughout time. I explain it in Step Nine.

5. Check out Emotional Freedom Technique (EFT), which involves tapping on "meridian points" on your body to release energy and reverse negativity. This is explained by an expert in Step Eight.

6. Again, I suggest seeking support if you feel like you need it. You must realize that your subconscious may fight to hold on to the old beliefs, because this is how it was trained to protect you. What you are doing is overriding your programming. Encountering others with similar struggles will strengthen your spirit because you'll know you're not alone. A therapist will be able to address your unique concerns and guide you.

# Objects

*"Acquisition is the root of suffering."*

—Buddha

What is it about humans that we cling to objects? This can certainly be understandable when we think of family photos or gifts from those we love. The problem stems from when we overcompensate by surrounding ourselves with objects, projecting emotions into them that simply do not exist. We run the risk of becoming engulfed by them—consumed in the piles that surround us.

This is worth a closer discussion about clutter.

## A NOTE FROM THE EXPERT: NINA CHMIEL

For some people, keeping your house organized is very easy. For others, not so much. (You already know which type you are.)

If you're a disorganized person, it's not difficult at all to change your habits, and the impact it will have on your level of comfort can't be overstated. It just takes being a bit more mindful of what you are doing. A lot of disorganized people are creative types who are a bit impatient and tend to move quickly from one activity to another. Taking a minute to make their bed in the morning, a few seconds to wipe the sink after they've used it, hang the towel up, or close the shampoo bottle all seem unnecessary and annoying to them. After a while, the house is in complete disarray, although they may be oblivious to the chaos because they're focused on their next project or endeavor. Add to that children, who are naturally moving quickly from one thing to another, and you have a major mess!

Sound like your home? Here's an idea: Designate the last fifteen minutes of each day to putting things back where they belong. If you have ice cream bowls over by the television, drink glasses, empty chip bags, art supplies, whatever, just put them back where they belong before you go to sleep. If you can get the whole family involved, it will be faster still. This way you will wake each morning to an organized home.

*Clutter:* Clutter is the enemy of a happy home. Think of clutter as thorns in your environment. It's prickly, sharp, and very uncomfortable, visually and physically.

Clutter usually accumulates first on the tops of furniture: Your nightstand, the top of your dresser, coffee table, kitchen counters, and bathroom vanity all are susceptible to clutter accumulations. If you see objects beginning to congregate in any of these places, stop and correct the problem before it gets out of hand. You should not have anything on the tops of your furniture that isn't part of your décor, and if your décor consists of more than one to two items on the top of anything, rethink the arrangement. Even bookshelves should have some open spaces and not be jam packed with books, the shelves sagging from the weight.

Closets and drawers are usually the recipients of the clutter that has accumulated. It's easy to throw things into a drawer or closet and close the door. Out of sight, out of mind. Although sooner or later, you know you'll have overstuffed closets and drawers. Better to decide if you really need the item before you stuff it in a drawer, and if you do, throw away something of equal size and weight that's already there. Some people can have serious issues purging items from their home, and if your accumulation of clutter is causing any concern, consider asking for professional help.

*Cleanliness:* It's not possible to live in a sterile environment, of course, but there are many things we can easily do to maintain a clean home. Years ago, my stay-at-home mother would constantly clean in a systematic way. First, she would dust everything including the floorboards and moldings, wipe underneath the sofa cushions with a damp rag to get rid of accumulated dirt, vacuum, and then polish. It was a process and ate up most of the day.

When I was an adult myself, I began to set aside each Saturday to do the same thing. I would clean my entire apartment and be left with little time to do anything else. I've gotten smarter since then, and now I know that cleaning doesn't have to be a whole day affair. Instead, I clean as I go along.

For most people, cleaning after meals is a given. But cleaning the bathroom, living areas, and bedrooms aren't as automatic. There are many cleaning hacks we can use today to clean as we go. My favorites are the automatic toilet cleaner tablets you put in the tank. These will give you a clean toilet for two to three months. My other favorite is the "clean shower" sprays you use each day after taking a shower. The throw-away wipes are great for wiping up the vanity each day, or even a roll of paper towels will do to wipe up after washing or brushing your teeth.

But my favorite go-to cleaning hack is actually a broom and dustpan. I keep a broom and dustpan handy on every floor of my house. Dirt tends to show up on floors first. Simply sweeping can greatly improve the appearance of your home. For carpets, I have a quick, cordless vacuum handy. It only takes a few seconds. Dusting with the new, throw-away dusters is fast and easy too. If you can clean as you go along each day, you'll always have a clean home.

Incorporating these ideas in your home is easy. And as we travel through life, in and out of spaces over which we have no control, it's nice to be able to return home to an oasis of calmness, order, serenity, and peace.

*After being honorably discharged from the United States Air Force, Nina Chmiel studied business and administrative management at St. Lawrence University in Quebec, Canada. In 1995, Nina left the investment banking industry to launch her own real estate business specializing in helping sellers and investors turn unappealing and distressed properties into desirable, attractive homes. Nina has consistently been counted among the top ten percent of real estate agents throughout the country. Nina has won numerous industry awards and has written several how-to books about preparing and selling real estate to maximize profits. Nina can be reached at NChmiel@hotmail.com and at Ninashomes.com.*

---

> *"Out of clutter,*
> *find simplicity.*
> *From discord,*
> *find harmony.*
> *In the middle of difficulty,*
> *lies opportunity."*

—Albert Einstein

Clutter comes in many degrees.

Do you have heaps of clothes you no longer wear, or stacks of magazines you'll never read?

Perhaps your junk drawer has expanded to several—it could be that random items are now piled on your counters and table.

Or maybe you are a packed-to-the-ceiling hoarder.

I think clutter is about avoidance. Trying to distract yourself from what is too hard and painful to deal with. It literally blocks your path and works as an amazing excuse for not dealing with the outside world.

When someone has so much to cope with inside their home, how can they begin to look on the outside?

The larger part of this is who the excuse is *really* aimed at.

It's aimed at yourself.

The bigger the problem you have with clutter, the more you are resisting taking a look at yourself. Perhaps you've bought books on de-cluttering; perhaps you've watched shows. But believe me, clutter is the symptom. You will never get past it if you don't recognize this: *Clutter is the tool you're using to deprive yourself of happiness because you're scared.*

---

## A NOTE FROM THE EXPERT: BRIAN REINTHALER

*"Minimalism is a tool that can assist you in finding freedom… freedom from the trappings of the consumer culture we've built our lives around."*

—Joshua Fields Millburn and Ryan Nicodemus, founders of theminimalists.com

I discovered minimalism in 2014.

That was the year I left corporate life to pursue work that better aligned with my skills and passions. I dove into a yearlong certification program as a life coach and launched my coaching practice. Throughout the year, I realized more and more that what makes me happy has very little connection to "things," and that often my emotional attachment to physical possessions was inhibiting my ability to envision and create the life I wanted.

Around the same time, my wife had begun merrily discarding objects from around our home and citing bloggers like Joshua Becker, who were then advocating for a burgeoning lifestyle movement in which people were getting rid of things that were not useful.

At first, these developments were not connected, but they dovetailed seamlessly. As we tightened our belts financially to smooth my professional transition and I got more in touch with what makes me (and my clients) happy, our family began prioritizing fulfilling life experiences over the acquisition and maintenance of material goods. And what we have learned since then has been as surprising as it has been fulfilling.

Minimizing possessions declutters more than just the home. My wife's "minimalizing" began with a few clothing donations, a garage sale, and the occasional purge of toys our girls no longer treasured. But when she set her sights on any of my things, I experienced considerable anxiety. As a recovering pack rat, I expressed some concerns:

*What if we wanted to watch TV in the other den?*

*But I spent years building that DVD collection!*

*I know I'm not practicing law anymore, but those law books look cool and reading them someday might make for good nostalgia.*

*What if we can use the furniture that's been gathering dust for five year in our next home?*

My materialist tendencies notwithstanding, I decided to dip my toe in this "minimalism" thing—we were contemplating a move, so getting of rid of *some* junk felt inevitable. As with anything, starting was the hard part. I would sit in contemplation of an item for half an hour, shifting back and forth between trash and treasure. Finally, I just grabbed something and chucked it.

What surprised me, though, was the small feeling of exhilaration as each item left my finger tips, bound for the bottom of a Hefty bag: a bobble-head doll and some ill-fitting corduroys here; a stack of old magazines there; a radio that hadn't been turned on since the Bush administration. This felt... good. And the more I tossed, the better it felt!

Within a few days, I couldn't help but notice—not only was our house becoming more livable, but my mind felt clearer. Ideas flowed more freely. Pretty soon, both a literal and a psychological weight had been lifted.

And then came another, even bigger surprise—I didn't even miss the things I discarded.

There may be nothing quite so liberating as unloading things that hold us back. The more stuff we have, the less we appreciate it. And devoting ourselves fully to the moment (and to the loved ones who inhabit them) is impossible when we're inundated and consumed by "things."

So if your goal is to enjoy *more* of your life, try committing to *less*. Less clutter. Fewer possessions. Maybe even a smaller budget? A smaller budget means fewer additional expenses, just like it would cost less money to decorate a small apartment than it would to decorate a large home.

The challenge is to distinguish the necessary, useful, and beautiful (the items that regularly bring us value or joy) from the balls and their chains. The physical and emotional space you create will far outweigh the value of the stuff that no longer occupies your life.

*Brian Reinthaler is a career transition and life coach who believes in challenging his clients to separate what they actually want from what they're "supposed to want" by empowering them to take charge of their lives and move confidently toward where they want to be. A graduate of The University of Notre Dame and Georgetown Law, Brian practiced corporate law in New York for four years and then spent seven years assisting lawyers seeking new jobs as a headhunter, before launching Against the Grain Coaching in 2014. Brian has recently served as a consultant to AltaClaro, heading up the development of continuing education and "soft" skills training programs for attorneys and compliance professionals. You can learn more about Brian at facebook.com/ATGCoach or email him at brian@atgcoach.com*

---

So, what can you do about all the clutter in your life?

*"Leap, and the net will appear."*

—John Burroughs

You're on a metaphorical airplane, and you're supposed to parachute out. But you don't want to! You're trembling; your heart palpitates.

There's a pile of junk in between you and the airplane door. Oh, well.

You can't jump after all. It's not your fault. You're blocked. The only thing you can do is start to rummage through the stuff, shifting little by oh-so-little. You use the excuse that maybe the stuff is valuable or cool. It's somehow important, even if you can't explain why. You can't just get rid of it. You need to examine it closely. You pick things up, push them around, look at them again—all without actually getting rid of even one item once and for all.

Why?

Because you don't really want to go through that door!

Jumping is scary.

You have a parachute. So what's the problem?

The problem is: Once you jump, it's up to you to pull that cord and release it. This is different than a net that appears on its own, isn't it? If you fail to pull that cord at the right time, you'll die. *Splat*.

So there's more than taking the leap and having faith. There's real work to be done—on you. But the good news is that you're totally capable of doing this work, and you don't have to rely on fate or faith to protect you.

The fact that you have to pull the parachute cord gives you an invincible power, as long as you push aside your pile of fear and get through that door.

You are your own net. Oh, how zen.

Acute hoarding is a sign of agony—someone who can't face the burden of life at all. It's so debilitating that a hoarder is assured to never have to deal with what's outside their home.

Hoarding things is an emotional substitution: If you put your emotions into objects—clinging to them with all of your might—you don't have to go out to meet your needs.

Also, these objects will never hurt your feelings or let you down.

The hardest part is admitting you have a problem—and that the problem is in your head and heart, not in the piles. You will probably need help. Please seek counseling.

Maybe you're related to a hoarder. Maybe you live with one. If at all possible, get out. Do not try to help them, unless they make a genuine request. Even then, say you'll give them one day to try and help. Do not feel guilty about not giving up more of your time. It's not your job to clean up their mess (literally or figuratively).

### Selene's Story

*I grew up with a hoarder—my mom. Though she saved many things, her particular focus was The New York Times. She saved every issue, insisting that she was going to read them. I never saw her read one. They were piled everywhere in the kitchen—on the counters, on the table, on the chairs. All the news that's fit to print was stacked under my butt.*

*She also bought clothes from the thrift shop and piled them in her room, on the bannister, and eventually in other rooms and down the stairs. There's something particularly upsetting about having the stairs cluttered and blocked.*

*She collected books—many, many books. But I never saw her read one. She had so many that she stored some in cardboard boxes on the front porch. They did not do well in the outdoors. We had rotting, smelly books.*

*She accumulated junk mail and also regular mail—often without opening it. Things built and built, and soon we were limited to the smallest path through the living room, inching our way through.*

*There was more, more, more…*

*I won't even describe the horror of the basement.*

*The few times I tried to clean, she freaked out—sometimes yelling, sometimes crying.*

*Sometimes she set out to "organize" in the night—but wound up fixated on one pile, examining things and never getting rid of one.*

*She even slept with piles of things on her bed, with just a small area for her to curl up in.*

*I moved out when I was eighteen.*

*But our childhood experiences define us. I found a partner who was also a hoarder!*

*When I saw the piles in his house, and going up the stairs, I had the distinct feeling that I was peering inside his brain. But instead of running, I forged ahead, trying to create a relationship with this man who had no clarity.*

*He moved into my house, and the hoarding there began. Inside, outside....*

*I could write a whole book about what he did to my beautiful, waterfront home. Here are just a few details:*

*He collected things from people's trash—most memorably, a Ms. Pac-Man machine. He perched it right on my deck, in the spot where I wrote! One of our cats found a way inside it, and she'd sleep among the wires.*

*He was into scrap metal, but wanted to compile enough to make a trip to the scrap yard worthwhile—and he also needed to separate it. So a corner of my yard became a scrap land. The image of a Nathan's hot dog cart umbrella atop a pile in my yard is forever etched in my mind. When I complained, he put a tarp over the metal.*

*He brought toilets and dumped them in my yard! They were too much for me, and I brought them to the dump myself.*

*He eventually built a garage-sized, tarp-enclosed structure, which he filled with tools, paint, more curbside garbage, bins and bins of who knew what... a complete wasteland, stretched across my yard.*

*Inside my house, he covered everything with junk, so that*

*it was impossible to have a family dinner—or a family anything. He bought a sectional couch from somewhere, but kept all the sections separate. He had about a million electronic gadgets piled up—some for his business and some just because.*

*Hurricane Sandy brought all this hoarding to an end, sweeping a tidal wave through my house and property. Ms. Pac-Man was carried into the neighbor's yard.*

*His electronics and tools were destroyed by the salt water—despite his attempts to save them with rice. (You cannot envision HOW MUCH RICE! Fifty pound satchels. To this day I am repulsed by rice.)*

*I also suffer from tarp PTSD. I get the shakes when I see one.*

*Once my space was cleaned up—about a year later!—I determined never to let hoarding happen in my space again.*

*And I didn't.*

## Concrete Action

# Clearing out the clutter

1. We get used to clutter, so much so that we fail to recognize it until we're faced with the arrival of a guest—and suddenly we're running around stuffing things into the closet. (And praying no opens that closet!) To see your home objectively, imagine yourself as a visitor

in your home. Now you can pick out the clutter with an unbiased, detached eye. You can also take pictures and imagine if they were posted on Facebook. What would your friends think about your living space?

2. The mistaken notion many of us have is that we need to clean out our closets and drawers to make room for the stuff laying around the house. I've attempted this, and wound up burning out and getting overwhelmed—and then I had more chaos because things from the closets and drawers were now out, too! Start with the visible clutter, and work your way into drawers and closets. But don't do more than a little bit every day, so you know you can complete the task. Pick one room, and stick with it daily until you're finished— and only then move on to another room. Pick one small task and do it—then congratulate yourself! (See Step Eight.) Repeat every day, and little by little you'll be clutter free!

3. Let go of any clothes you haven't worn in a year. Either donate them to charity, or give them away to someone you know. There are also local Facebook groups and even apps devoted to "swapping and shopping." It depends how much time you're willing to invest.

4. Hang up all the clothes you want to keep without sorting them into sections—just go through the piles rapidly and deposit them in the closet. The nice looking row will make you feel accomplished, and you can organize them into sections at a later date. If you get distracted by interior closet organizing, you'll burn out before getting the exterior organizing done—and you might have a bigger mess to contend with than before!

5. Emotional attachment to items is the hardest thing to break free of. I was attached to my kids' stuffed animals because I associated them with my kids themselves. I allowed myself to save a couple in the closet and took pictures of the rest. Then I gave them away to another child.

6. Taking a picture of something you cherish is a great way to keep a memory without having to keep the actual item. Like that '80s fringed leather jacket you bought because Jon Bon Jovi had one.

And thanks to modern technology, you can keep your pictures stored virtually! You can also post them on Facebook, and invite your friends to share their out-of-the-closet nostalgia.

7.  You can preserve and honor notes, cards, ticket stubs, programs, and any "stray" paper memories you have in piles and drawers by mounting them in shadow boxes. How about laminating them (you can buy an inexpensive laminating machine) and then hanging them on a decorative corkboard. You can even mount cork and decorate your walls with your mementos! Or you can scrapbook (beware: this does take time if you're tempted to get all fancy with the pages, like I did when my kids were little)—or buy decorative boxes (they come in all sizes and shapes now) and store your mementos in them. But be careful not to get all caught up in sorting for the boxes. You want to tackle the outside clutter first!

8.  Find a book on decluttering which appeals to you. The recent one by Marie Kondo is listed in my "further reading" section—but there are so many. Browse through your library or bookstore, or scroll around Amazon to find the perfect one for you!

9.  Celebrate yourself after each day's accomplishment! (See Step Eight.) Have a ceremony where you officially bid the things you no longer need goodbye, while welcoming the next chapter of your life. You can incorporate candles, sage, music, and anything else that appeals to you.

# DO WHAT MAKES YOU HAPPY

here are two main reasons to do what makes you happy:

1. You have purpose

2. You have passion

*"Purpose is the reason you journey.*
*Passion is the fire that lights the way."*

—Anonymous

---

*"Your purpose in life is to find your purpose and give your whole heart and soul to it"*

—Buddha

## Purpose

To have purpose means you are driven. You are focused in a direction.

*"The purpose of life is a life of purpose."*

—Robert Byrne

*"Anything that gets your blood going is probably worth doing."*

—Hunter S. Thompson

## FROM THE DOCTOR'S DESK: LINDSAY S. WEISNER, PSY.D

I fell in love with psychology when I was sitting in an environmental biology class. I didn't intend on finding something to date, never mind fall in love with and eventually marry. (I was only in the right place at the right time because I needed to fulfill a freshman year science requirement.)

The class focused on the similarities, rather than the differences, that exist across species: We are all animals attempting to survive, both as individuals, and as an attempt to further the species. And the vast majority of our behaviors—both good and bad—can be linked back to this survival instinct.

(And yeah, I still think back to this class when I am working with patients today.)

By the end of the year, I had made the decision to transfer schools and change majors. My sophomore year psychology classes deepened my love for the field and provided me with a glimpse into my psyche. (I learned all the things that were messed up about me and my family. Mind. Blown.)

But the thing that really put the ring on my finger was when the psychology professor that I loved and adored informed me—in no uncertain terms—that I should not bother with psychology because I would probably never do anything with the degree.

And yet, I do.

According to Sigmund Freud, the therapist should be a "blank slate," about whom you know nothing. The therapist should have no problems, no feelings, no family, and no form. If a patient asks any questions of a personal nature, I am to interpret their curiosity as a part of their psychological make-up. Through this lens, the therapist is intended to be viewed as a sort of paused entity who lives only within the four walls of the office and serves merely to help you reflect on your past, organize your thoughts, and interpret your behavior. No more and no less.

For example: a young woman comes to therapy because the birth of her second child has brought on feelings of hopelessness and helplessness. She spends her first session in tears, asking repeatedly if it is "normal" for her to have these feelings, which at times make her wonder if her life would be better if she hadn't had a second child. At the end of the session, as we are scheduling our next appointment, she asks me if I have children, and if I think she is an awful person for feeling so "depressed" when she has this beautiful, healthy baby boy at home.

How would Freud suggest I respond to this patient in her time of need?

"Why don't we talk some more about that next week," or "What would it mean to you if I did have children? Or, perhaps, if I did not?" or "It sounds like you are looking for some reassurance that it is okay to feel the way that you do."

Yet how do I respond? "I do have children. And I remember when my son was born, I was so overwhelmed and sleep-deprived that the only way I could keep track of night and day was by raising my blinds in the morning and lowering them at night. And I also know that it will get better. We will get you through this."

*Oof.* Did you hear that? That was the sound of the door being slammed as Freud kicked me out of his school.

I interrupt a little more than I probably should, and I tend to punctuate my speech with four-letter words a teensy bit more than any educated, professional woman should.

If you are my patient, I will not mince words. I will tell you when you are wrong, and I will be the first to emphatically agree that what your new boss said to you is "super fucked up."

My patients know that I have two young children, that I live in the same town in which my office is located, and that my family has managed to murder five goldfish in the last four weeks.

So why all the cursing and chaos?

Like I said, I'm not very good at my job—but I'm damn good at my purpose. And I have no doubt that helping people is what I was put on this Earth to do.

This job is tough. Really tough. I know, I know, what's so tough about sitting in an office listening to people talk?

Everything.

A therapist is a container for everyone else's shitty emotions. Fear, anger, anxiety, sadness, confusion—you name it, I take it and hold it for you. And for everyone else I see that day, week, month, and year. At the end of the day, I'm exhausted.

But having a purpose—having *this* purpose—this purpose gives me incredible strength.

And science backs me up on this one. Did you know that money can, in fact, buy happiness? Yup. But only if you give that money away. People who regularly donate to non-profit organizations—especially religious organizations—are happier. Maybe this is because happiness tends to come from what a Harvard study called "the three goods": doing good for others, doing good for themselves, and doing things that they are good at.

Do you see what these three goods have in common? They all allow the individual doing the good to take on an identity of some sort, whether that identity, or role, is how other people as a whole will view them or how they will be able to identify, or classify, themselves.

The wealthy older man who is always quick to pull out his checkbook for the children's hospital will be admired by many and thought of as the charitable benefactor. The woman who is finally strong enough to leave her verbally abusive spouse has done something good for herself, and she will soon become a beacon of strength for those struggling to rid themselves of a similar burden. Lastly, of course, the athletes or actors who succeed in their chosen career will be known for their statistics or statues above all else.

Each of these three "goods" carry along with them a sense of identity or purpose that falls across the brow of the individual in question. And is it any wonder that this sense of purpose appears to contribute to happiness?

Positive Psychology is a relative newcomer to the field, and proponents aim to highlight the good, positive aspects of both individuals and society as a whole. The emphasis is on positive experiences, like happiness and love; positive traits, like resiliency and compassion; and the bigger question of how can we apply the experience of the individual to the community at large.

Stop pointing out deficiencies and diseases and start paying attention to how people make the best out of disheartening situations.

And guess what? Attending to the positive and finding meaning in your life comes with amazing mental and physical health benefits. People who believe that their lives have meaning and purpose tend to experience less stress and improved coping skills following physical ailments and/or surgery, which resulted in better physical health after surgery.

People who feel that their life has purpose—either individual or vicarious purpose—tend to take better care of themselves. Older adults tend to move more, which is super-important, because physical activity is highly correlated with overall health and wellbeing.

I believe that successful therapy demands that you, the patient, rip your heart out of your chest and wear it on your sleeve, your shirt, your pants, and the floor of my office. But in order to do this, you have to feel comfortable baring your soul.

I wouldn't want to bare my soul to a blank slate. Would you? Would Freud? Would anyone?

I can help you to understand how and why your past keeps fucking up your current job and your last four relationships. Trust me, if you don't get a hold of your past, it's going to continue to destroy your future.

Together, we will find your purpose. We will figure out what will make you want to wake up in the mornings. We will figure out what ideas you can wonder about as you fall asleep at night—rather than tossing and turning while your anxiety keeps you and your pillow company.

Your purpose will become a hell of a lot clearer once you stop revisiting the highlight reel of disappointments and failures from your past.

Maybe you'll even start getting rid of those destructive, distractive relationships.

Maybe you'll get out of your own way long enough to find a way to be happy.

---

*"Everyone has been made for some particular work and the desire for that work has been put in every heart."*

—Rumi

---

## A NOTE FROM THE EXPERT: DANIEL LAMAS

So many people have jobs that they absolutely hate in order to make ends meet. I am fortunate enough to be able to make a living in my field, and a rather good one at that. And I could not imagine myself doing anything else.

As a performer, you give your audience everything you have on stage. I tell my audience a story from my point of view, but it is entirely possible that the audience may come up with a different story. Often times after concerts, I've met audience members who tell me that the performance took them back to a childhood memory, a distant land, or even served as some sort of comfort. I remember once playing a chamber music concert and shaking hands with one person who just said "thank you" with their eyes glistening. Then and there, I knew that what I did had a greater purpose than any monetary or egocentric end.

In my career, I have often encountered people who love to perform, but hate to teach. There are always students and situations that make you want to scream and break something, but then there are times when the student finally understands and progress is made.

The formula for success is what I call the "Holy Trinity": the teacher, the student, and the adult in charge, all working as a team. This is how a student makes significant process.

Being an educator is much more than just teaching someone a skill set. When I was young, my teacher, Michael Klotz, became like a big bother to me. We are still very close, and I still seek his counsel on musical matters from time to time. He taught me how to play the violin, and then the viola, and then taught me how to live like an artist. He made sure I kept on top of my studies, both musical and academic. He was quick to scold me if I did anything stupid. And he was the first one to praise me for an achievement.

This is the type of person I strive to be with each of my students. And the relationship doesn't end when the lessons end. Many of my former students still keep me updated on their lives. And to know that I've made a positive impact on their lives, that is by far the greatest reward.

*Daniel Lamas is a violist, violinist, and educator. Apart from performing with different ensembles in the U.S. and abroad, he is the director of the Roosevelt Island Music Studio. Daniel can be reached at dlamasmusic@gmail.com.*

*"The soul which has no fixed purpose in life is lost; to be everywhere, is to be nowhere."*

—Michel de Montaigne

It is almost impossible to be unhappy while you're immersed in your true purpose. (The key is immersion—you must be steeped in it, and sometimes it is our faltering and failure to jump into the "deep end" that makes us unhappy. More on that later.)

> *"It's not enough to have lived.*
> *We should be determined to live for something."*
>
> —Leo Buscaglia

When we don't have a purpose in our work, we may try to get it another way. This pursuit often heightens to a frenzy, maybe even an obsession. Some people obsess over order or cleanliness. Some delve into volunteer work. I'm not saying there's anything wrong with order, cleanliness, or volunteering. I'm saying it's the lengths people go to doing it which can be troublesome, because they're trying to force something to be fulfilling when it's just not. If something truly makes you happy, you will have an ease with it. You'll know it's right. There will be no struggle, no grappling. It is like falling in love. In fact, it *is* falling in love. Not infatuation, not a crush. Love.

> *"Musicians must make music,*
> *artists must paint,*
> *poets must write*
> *if they are ultimately to be at peace with themselves.*
> *What humans can be, they must be."*
>
> —Abraham Maslow

> *"The mystery of human existence lies not in just staying alive, but in finding something to live for."*
>
> —Fyodor Dostoyevsky,
> *The Brothers Karamazov*

*"The meaning of life is to find your gift. The purpose of life is to give it away."*

—Pablo Picasso

*"True happiness… is not attained through self-gratification, but through fidelity to a worthy purpose."*

—Helen Keller

---

## A NOTE FROM THE EXPERT: BETH STAR

I was thirteen years old when I realized fashion was an armor I could hide behind—if done correctly.

I remember the outfit that inspired me: The sweater (it was probably hideous) was red, blue, and yellow, and I struggled to decide which socks would be the way to go. I remember asking my mother if I could wear two different socks, and she just kind of shrugged and said, "Sure, why not. You can do anything you want to."

Actually, there were a hell of a lot of reasons why not, although I wasn't brave enough to voice any of these reasons to my mother. In school, I had always been a wallflower, not a trendsetter. The idea of wearing two different-colored socks to school was bold and beyond me in a way that my mother couldn't possibly understand.

Although my mom always makes a point of looking damn good, she has never been super-into fashion or following trends. At the time, she was too busy raising my two brothers and me. The three of us were a handful, always pulling her in different directions with our bold desires and wanton opinions. My parents did not believe in raising meek children.

My father has always been artistic, and although he has used many different mediums over the years, the sketches from my childhood of my brothers and me having all sorts of adventures—both real and imagined—still stick in my mind. He is also good at math and numbers, which made his career as an optometrist and eyeglasses store owner a perfect fit for him.

It took me a little longer to find my perfect fit. But I guess in some ways, it's the journey that takes you where you really need to be.

Looking back, I think I realized from a pretty young age that fashion for me was about finding something to wear that made me feel good about *me*. And if it made me feel good, it was probably going to make other people feel good too.

Don't get me wrong, I absolutely look back at some pictures from my past and cringe thinking about what I was wearing and how I was feeling.

(Especially old pictures from the '80s. That was a rough time, fashion-wise—for all of us, I would like to think. Dear God, those poofy shoulders and stirrup pants, and those high-waisted pants and so-cool body suits that were a great idea in theory and somehow failed most of us in fit.)

I love fashion, but it wasn't until I was asked to write this piece that I truly realized how much I have come to depend on my clothing as armor, of sorts. Over the last few years there have been plenty of times when it has helped to focus on looking good on the outside when I wasn't feeling so great on the inside.

I remember there was a man I dated shortly before I met my husband. I was young and foolish enough to believe that I had to fit into a mold that was so much more conservative than I was. And much, much, much more conservative than the person I am today. I was head-to-toe Brooks Brothers and Hermès, and although that experience taught me the important life lesson that fifteen minutes at a good tailor is outfit-changing, I left that relationship with the urge to break out of conservative and comfortable and safe.

And that's the person I am today.

Every day I try to make an effort to feel less conservative. When people compliment me, it gives me the strength and confidence to experiment more. I tell my friends and my customers to push the limits and go outside their comfort zone and see how it makes them feel.

Very rarely do people feel worse for being brave.

That whole "fake it 'til you make it" thing really sticks in my head as I am writing this.

Two years ago, I ended my career of seventeen years with no path carved out for my future. I can honestly say that those first few months were the saddest I have ever been in my life. It felt like I was leaving my small-town high school to choose what my life would be like all over again.

I faked it and smiled at my friends, family, and acquaintances for weeks on end.

And then my husband reminded me of a secret that I had confided in him during our engagement: When Gregg and I were getting married, my husband really wanted to be able to give me my dream wedding. He lovingly murmured in my ear that every woman has been dreaming of her wedding since she was a little girl, and I more than anyone deserved my dream wedding.

It was really, really, really sweet.

And it was really, really, really not true.

For as long as I can remember, the day I had been looking forward to was when my best friend and I opened our store, "Mom's Closet." My fantasies involved the day my imaginary store opened. Not my wedding day.

And it was this nudge, this reminder, this teasing from the man who had known me for three years that made everything clear.

I had gone to culinary school and worked in the restaurant business for nine years, bringing me to twenty-eight. I was well-versed in presentation and the hospitality business. I had worked in a high-end eyeglass boutique for seventeen years in a role that was more friend and personal shopper than retail employee.

And at forty-three years of age, perched at the edge of this devastating crossroad in my life, I knew what I loved and I knew what I wanted to do: it was time for me to open my store, my way.

Looking back, "Mom's Closet" wasn't about the cool clothes our parents were wearing; it was simply about being able to pick and choose the best of what someone else has. That's how I manage my business now. A lot of items I only carry in one brand, because it is the brand that I have thoroughly researched enough to be comfortable calling it the best. For example, I'm loving 143 t-shirts, Sheridan Mia shoes, and Green Roads CBD.

### *Any fashion advice?*

Invest in a good blazer, immediately. A blazer is a piece of clothing that is worth spending a bit more on, since it can be worn in a million different ways. The value is in the versatility. A blazer can dress up sweatpants or jeans and sneakers, or you can wear it more conservatively, over a little black dress or with dress pants. Personally, I'm a big fan of Elias Rumelis blazers. These are classically styled but have sporty and feminine details.

I like finding new things that fit people in a way that challenges their previously-held beliefs of what they "can" wear. People really do come in all shapes and sizes. And take my word for it—everyone has something about their body that they don't like. You can't work against it, but you can work around it and find comfort in it.

Larger hips? Don't try to cover them or tuck in a form-fitting shirt. Look for a longer shirt or a looser, blousier top. There is truly nothing that a good duster can't hide.

*(Editor's note for the fashion-impaired: a duster is just a long shirt that you can wear unbuttoned or unzipped; and according to our guest writer, a "duster" is always going to be in fashion because of how flattering it is.)*

Another problem area for most women—especially those over thirty-five—is breasts. Too small for some, too big for others, and if you have anything above a B-cup and you have had a child, then you probably hate having to wear a bra all day as much as I do. But life dictates that I have to factor a good bra into anything I wear. So I work with it by opting for the best fitting—which usually means the most expensive—bras I can find.

When you get dressed, the biggest part of you looking good is feeling good. It's okay to have fat clothes in your closet. Sometimes I get the most compliments on my so-called fattest days. It's okay to feel fat. Just dress accordingly. Some of my fattest days, scale-wise, are accompanied by the biggest compliments.

Find a company that works for you and your body, and stick with it. Day to day clothing doesn't need tailoring; special events, make sure the dress fits you. Don't try to fit into the dress.

*Beth Star received her training from the French Culinary Institute in New York City and spent seventeen years at a boutique store where she cultivated an eyewear collection that brought her a client following from all over the country. She is married to the most conservative man on the planet who doesn't like change, which is remarkable considering how much Beth enjoys change. She has two amazing and amusing daughters, and her home is filled with more animals than she knows what to do with. For more about her fashion sense, visit ajandmos.com, follow her on Instagram @ajandmos, or email her at ajandmos@gmail.com.*

---

# Passion

*"Every great dream begins with a dreamer. Always remember, you have within you the strength, the patience, and the passion to reach for the stars to change the world."*

—Harriet Tubman

Everybody has a dream. And that dream is your passion.

But so many of us avoid that dream, or pretend they don't know what it is. Maybe when you were young you were put down for that dream, or convinced that it could never happen. Maybe you wiped it right out of your mind—selective amnesia. Or maybe you cradle it deep inside your heart, waiting for the right time. What time is more right than now? Why wait to pursue your passion?

*"Passion will move men beyond themselves, beyond their shortcomings, beyond their failures."*

—Joseph Campbell

*"Finding your passion isn't just about careers and money. It's about finding your authentic self. The one you've buried beneath other people's needs."*

—Kristin Hannah, *Distant Shores*

Do something you love—whether you intend to make a living from it or not! Not sure of your passion? Then explore different things. You'll never know what you love if you don't look for it. Or maybe you do know your passion, but something keeps you from pursuing it. You must!

Why is your passion so vital? Because it is your personal truth.

*"And you will know the truth, and the truth will set you free."*

—The Bible, John 8:32

I'll modify this to say: "YOUR truth shall set you free."

Finding happy requires embracing your unique authenticity and not caring what anyone else thinks.

It's easy to be sidetracked from your passion, or even to miss out on finding it at all. Too many people waste their lives with their heads metaphorically buried in the sand—buried by other people's agendas. There will always be false trails and dead ends. When you live your life according to your truth—when you follow your true path and not someone else's—you'll find a peace like no other.

Don't know your passion? Get out there and explore! It's so easy to learn about things these days, either in person or through the internet.

## Selene's Story

*My son Michael was in his middle school chorus. He really sang his heart out—just put everything he had into it. The teachers weren't used to such passion. One actually called me to tell me that Michael was mocking the performance, because he was swaying and smiling and belting out the words. I told her it was exuberance. A shame it's not recognizable!*

## FROM THE DOCTOR'S DESK: LINDSAY S. WEISNER, PSY.D

If you're doing it right, it should come as no surprise that sex makes people happy. First, you know, orgasm. Duh. And even if you don't have an orgasm, the very act of physical activity gets your endorphins pumping. (Pun intended).

Also, sex with someone that you lust after, like, or love can feel like the best form of flattery, as long as your expectations are realistic.

And guess what? Research shows that the relationship between sex and happiness defies health status, gender, and age.

Yup. Sexually transmitted diseases and nursing homes go hand in hand for a reason: happiness. Older adults (think seventy and above) who engage in regular sexual activity are more likely to report a better quality of life and better interpersonal relationships.

It almost sounds like this book could have been a lot shorter, and we could have just called it: *"One Step to Finding Happy: Get Naked a Whole Bunch."*

But it doesn't really work like that.

In 2015, a study came out that analyzed the responses of 31,000 people about how often they had sex, and how happy they believed they were. (This is an enormous number of people for a scientific study to use, so we can be pretty certain that the science here is legitimate.)

Wanna know what they discovered?

## Finding #1: Having sex regularly is related to happiness—but not if you are single.

There is often a grass-is-greener mentality that strikes both the Single and Hitched alike during certain developmental stages in life. This is especially true during times of change or transition.

The reality is that being single carries with it a certain kind of freedom to do what you want, whether that means staying out drinking until four in the morning or heading to the gym for a midnight sweat session. On the other hand, the comfort and security that comes along with a committed relationship means that "Netflix and chill" is more about relaxing and less about remembering to shave your legs.

So how come sex is correlated with the happiness of people in relationships, but not people who are single and free to sow their oats as they please?

Perhaps the happiness that surpasses post-coital pleasure may be more related to intimacy and familiarity than kink and orgasm. (Which is not to say that you can't have kink and familiarity—it's a combination we highly recommend.)

What does this mean for you?

1. If you are in a relationship, make sure you keep the physical connection alive. Prioritize sex even if your busy job or noisy children or nosy in-laws seem to dampen the mood. Sometimes this may mean having sex when you don't quite feel up to it. So if you're bloated or tired or haven't shaved your legs in two weeks—do it anyways. There's a good chance you'll feel better when you do.

2. If you are single, casual sex can be a fun distraction, but if you think you will find happiness at the bottom of the empty box of condoms, it's unlikely to happen.

## Finding #2: More sex isn't related to more happiness.

Couples in a committed relationship who have sex on a regular basis tend to be happier than couples in committed relationships who do not have sex on a regular basis. But, contrary to our cultural mindset, more isn't always better.

Why?

When it comes to sex and happiness, it's not just about frequency. The quality of the sex—both in terms of mind-blowing orgasms and emotional intimacy—matters as well.

A couple that has sex four to five times a week may be doing so because they are *amazing* at having sex together. Or they may be doing so because they are just that truly, madly, deeply in love the way we all dreamt about right before we got our braces off. Or maybe they just really want to piss off their nosy neighbors, and hey, sex seems like a hell of a good way to do so.

And then there is the couple that has sex four to five times a week because one of them is desperately trying to salvage the love that is waning, or to establish an emotional intimacy that simply isn't there.

I talk about sex with my patients a lot. I make a point to ask the tough, weird questions about the subjects that we only talk about with our closest girlfriends. If I don't ask, I'm just nodding my head and assuming that what I think of as good sex or rough sex or quick sex is the same thing you think of. And odds are, it's not.

A lot of my female patients wish they were having more sex in their relationship. But why? Is it simply about the all-mighty O and the woman simply has a higher sex drive? It's possible. But the vast majority of us learned to masturbate when we hit puberty. So if it's an issue of a difference in sex drives, why not simply take matters in your own hand (pun *totally* intended) and take some pressure off your relationship.

In my experience, usually the whole "higher sex drive" excuse is not about a physical need, but an emotional one.

The truth is—and this one is fairly predictable—women tend to equate sex with love more often than men. And yeah, it's probably in part due to the whole oxytocin thing, plus the societal expectation of women as pure and virginal. And yeah, the sexual revolution of every one of the last five decades has totally given us the girl power to go *grrr* and get what we need, sexually.

But, biologically, there is still that thing, where women get stuck holding the bag—the bag that contains the baby. Literally. For nine months. So, it make sense that women would be conditioned by nature (some sort of inherent gene-type thingy) or by nurture (a.k.a. society) to place more importance on the emotional attachment to intercourse.

What does this mean for you?

If you and your partner are having sex regularly (let's say one to two times a week) but one of you is constantly left wanting more, go ahead and flatter or be flattered (depending on your role in the twosome). But don't forget to give some thought to whether there is something else you need more of, besides sex. If something is lacking or waning, or a fear or anxiety is invading the safety of your relationship, it makes sense that the desire to increase intimacy will pop up, like an emotional security system. "Uh oh! Uh oh! Have more sex! There is a problem with your relationship!"

Sex is fantastic. But it isn't a substitute for the emotional intimacy that your relationship may be lacking.

# The Time of Your Life

*"All we have to decide is what to do with the time that is given us."*

—J.R.R. Tolkien,
*The Fellowship of the Ring*

Another reason to do what you love is that your job is the thing you spend most of your time doing—and when you're not at work, it's still on your mind. Why would you want to spend all those hours of your life doing something you don't like?

*"It is not that we have so little time but that we lose so much… The life we receive is not short but we make it so; we are not ill provided but use what we have wastefully."*

—Seneca

On the flip-side, the march of time and the need to work—because, let's face it, making money isn't optional—can become monotonous. Read on for Elora Philbrick's thoughts on finding happiness in the small, every-day moments.

---

## A NOTE FROM THE EXPERT: ELORA PHILBRICK

I grew up in a small town in New Hampshire surrounded by towering trees and an abundance of cow farms. The closest mall was over an hour away. My family has always been blue-collar, and my parents have always worked hard to provide my sister and me with every opportunity they did not have. Money was tight, which meant that I learned the importance of money at a very young age.

One summer, I convinced my already-financially-struggling parents to purchase a set of encyclopedias from a door-to-door salesman who pulled into our dirt driveway. The books were $500 for a set of five, and my parents paid for the entire set. Between us, the books were not used as much as they should have been, but that purchase always reminds me of just how dedicated my parents were to providing us with a better future.

I remember how difficult it was for my family to pay bills at the end of the month. Sometimes there wasn't enough money to go around. Sometimes the date of the paycheck didn't line up with the due date of the bills. Often times we struggled.

But my parents made it clear that fiscal responsibility was not only important, but there was also a satisfaction from making small sacrifices in the short term to lead to greater happiness in the long run.

I don't know anyone who likes to pay bills. You are suddenly forced to watch all of your hard-earned money diminish before you can even blink twice.

You are probably asking yourself right now, "How could it be possible to be happy while paying my bills?"

***Bills are the price of admission we pay
for a lifetime of experiences....***

Well, it may be a stretch to think that you would happily relinquish all of your cash when a piece of paper sent through the mail orders you to do so. But if you change your perspective, you may be happy... or at least happier.

The next time you feel the weight of unpaid bills heavily on your chest, take a moment to think about what each of those pieces of paper actually represent.

My parents accepted a few months of financial insecurity and a temporary increase in debt in order to educate their children. The money spent on the encyclopedias was worth it because those encyclopedias made my sister and me feel special. That money helped us to understand more about how and why the world works the way it does. The bill for those books was an investment in that it furthered our interest in school and resulted in a better education for us.

And that monthly student loan bill that will be with *you* a lot longer than your carefree youth? Yes, it feels like a horrible hassle that will never be paid off, but really, it's a trade-off for the memories you made with your friends and roommates.

A memory from college is well-worth financial debt? Well, what about that time I saved a friend's life.

One night as I was getting ready for bed, two of my friends came running through the door. The first girl—my roommate—looked terrified. Then my second friend stumbled in. Her face was purple, and she wasn't breathing. I managed to help her into a chair, and my roommate quickly explained she was having an allergic reaction to something she had eaten. My roommate had an EpiPen for her own allergies, but she was too frightened to use it on anyone else. Instead, she shoved the EpiPen into my hands.

Fortunately, I had spent several years as a camp counselor, and I was familiar with the device. I kneeled down and rolled up my friend's yoga pants to her thigh. Her frightened blue eyes looked back at me as I told her to hold still then injected her with the life-saving medication.

Almost immediately, her face became pink again, and she began panting. I had never actually seen anyone's face turn blue until that night, and I can't imagine what could have happened if I hadn't been there. Things could have turned out very differently that night, but thanks to my student loans, I was there to save her life. And to me, that is something worth paying for.

### *I guess this is growing up….*

In order to maintain all those bill payments, you have to work. Working a full-time job, or even a part-time job, takes time away from family, pets, as well as all of the other things you would rather be doing. Similarly to paying your bills, you must think about all of the good reasons why you work rather than focusing solely on the bad.

My current job at Fidelity allows me to help set people up for success once they reach retirement age. Aside from what I've learned about their unique personal lives, I've also learned a great deal about finances, which has helped to bring me the insight used in writing this piece. I never thought that working as a 401K Associate would turn into an opportunity that landed me here.

You have to remember that the money you make working does not just keep food on the table. Even if it is not your dream job, it is changing you in ways you may never have realized, whether that's helping you to grow into someone greater or allowing you to help others to do so.

Outside of looking at the bigger picture, there are additional techniques to incorporating pleasure at work, like placing photos of what or who motivates you on your desk or using them as your screensaver. Another research-proven way to improve your mood at work is by incorporating the color blue, whether it's through photographs or office supplies. According to Nancy Kwallek, PhD, a professor at the University of Texas, the color blue has a calming effect in the workplace that helps promote stimulation and productivity. By including the color blue in your workspace, you will be increasing happiness by reducing stress.

### You can't be pitiful AND be powerful

Mornings can be tough, but never forget that you are tougher. With mornings come obnoxious alarm clocks, dragging grunting teenagers from their beds, traffic, as well as trying to get toddlers dressed (and keeping them dressed).

But don't let yourself be blinded by the ugliness of mornings.

Don't forget the warm embrace from your hot cup of coffee. My favorite spot is a coffee shop set up in the shell of a former Taco Bell—complete with the light blue and purple paint scheme of the fast food joint in the '90s. The idea of this has always reminded me of a hermit crab leaving its shell for someone else to take up residence. I find it quaint and quite honestly think they have the best donuts around, which of course is an added bonus to the coffee.

If I have to come in to work particularly early, I let myself splurge on coffee and donuts as I sneak in a few feel-good stretches and enjoy the few minutes of quiet before the world starts.

Remind yourself to take the time to enjoy these often-forgotten pleasures of morning—even if you're not a morning person. You are still going to have to drag yourself out of bed, maybe for a job that wasn't your dream. But a favorite coffee spot can provide a moment or two of pleasure.

Focus on sneaking in small moments of happy into the dreary, daily tasks of your day. This way, you can re-train your brain to think of paying bills as a barter system that allows you to have the experiences you want. Work gives you money for those experiences that bring you joy. And even if the job you have isn't the one you wanted, always remember to take advantage of it, keep your eyes open and learn everything you can—you'll probably learn some things you didn't expect!

If you do this a little bit every day, you can bring happiness into the boring and mundane tasks of life.

*Elora Philbrick is a graduate of Franklin Pierce University and received her BA in English and mass communications. She has been published in* An Anthology of Emerging Poets 2017 *by Z Publishing House, and was awarded the Harriet Wilson Fiction Prize in 2016. Elora has experience in writing, editing, publishing, journalism reporting and investigative journalism. Currently, she resides in New Hampshire and can be contacted at ephilbrick96@gmail.com.*

*"It is never too late to be what you might have been."*

—George Eliot

## Concrete Action

# Do what makes you happy

1.  Write down a detailed description of what you do for a living. Describe everything you like and don't like. Explain why you chose this career. Do you feel it gives you purpose? Is it your passion? If yes, congratulations! Move on to our next step! If no…

2.  Define your purpose and your passion. If you think you don't have either, dig deeper. Think about the things you're drawn to. Books, movies, people, schools of thought… anything and everything is a clue to what you're meant to do, to become! There's a book called *What Color is Your Parachute?* that is designed to help people discover their passion. Check it out!

3.  Journal on this: What would it take to become the thing you are supposed to be?

4.  Visualize yourself in the role you are meant to be in.

5.  Make a day-by-day schedule of small tasks you can complete toward reaching your goal. This is so you don't get overwhelmed. If you break up anything into small pieces, it becomes comfortable and manageable. How long will it take you to get to that place? If you're going back to school, break this into steps that make sense for your situation. But small steps are possible: one day, you can research programs; another day, you can make a list of application deadlines or any pertinent information you need for each school. Then, each day, focus on one application. One day's task can be applying for financial aid or researching various ways of getting loans. You can do this!

6.  Carry out your schedule, all the while taking time to be grateful for the process and visualizing yourself at your goal.

Even if you can't quit your current job for financial reasons, you can still pursue your passion. We have time for what we make time for; if it's important to us, we can find a way. The important thing is to begin, and the adrenaline will flow!

## STEP SEVEN

# BELIEVE IN YOUR DREAMS AND TAKE ACTIVE STEPS IN PURSUING THEM

Once you're on the road to what makes you happy, you must continue full steam ahead. Never take it for granted, and never stop pursuing more growth and knowledge.

Sometimes you start off full blast, energized by your new awareness and resolution. You are thrilled that you have a path to follow—a goal to reach!

But once the novelty and adrenaline wear off, and you're in your routine, you may find enthusiasm to be challenging at times. You may also become overwhelmed by the enormity of your task, or frustrated, or scared.

FROM THE DOCTOR'S DESK: LINDSAY S. WEISNER, PSYD

What is resiliency?

Resiliency is the ability to bounce back when something bad happens. Someone who gets a speeding ticket on the way to work and allows this to ruin their whole day can be thought of as not being very resilient. Whereas someone who gets a speeding ticket on the way to work, accidentally locks themselves out of the house, forgets to attend an important work meeting, and still comes home with a smile—that would be someone with a great deal of resiliency.

Resiliency is also defined as the ability of an object to spring back into shape, also known as elasticity. Personally, this is the definition to which I have always been partial, particularly when it comes to survivors of trauma. I like the idea that even individuals who have been subject to war and assault and abuse have the ability to spring back into place, given enough time and care and desire.

No matter what you have come from, or what you are dealing with now, your ability to recover from life's setbacks—both large and small—is a huge component of your happiness. How can you become more resilient?

Dr. Kenneth Ginsburg created the 7 Cs model of resiliency as a guide for parents to help teach their children resiliency. If we can teach it to children, we can certainly try to improve on this skill within ourselves.

# Competence

Our ability to feel good about ourselves is not just based on what we can do well in one specific area. But feeling good about one thing you do well can lead to you feeling good in other areas. Be brave. Try new things. Sometimes you will surprise yourself by being amazing. Other times you will surprise yourself by failing miserably. But win or lose, you will learn more about yourself. Which means you will learn to trust yourself more.

# Confidence

Put yourself out there. Congratulate yourself for your accomplishments. Celebrate yourself. Write them down in your notebook and force yourself to acknowledge your success. And don't be afraid to brag about yourself. Sometimes saying it out loud to someone else can make the amazingness of what you have done feel more real.

# Connection

People need people, no matter their age. Focus on your people—the ones you call crying and laughing and screaming. They are the ones that will help you bounce back from the crap life throws at you. Being part of a group is another great idea to foster resiliency skills. Join a club, hang out in a Facebook group that interests you, or become more active in your religious organization. It helps.

# Character

Who are you, and what is most important to you? Is it career? Family? Being a caretaker to an ailing parent? This isn't about what you *should* do or who you *should* be. I hate when people use the word "should." Why? Because it always sounds like some sort of punitive parent who sets rigid expectations that are a struggle to live up to. Instead, defining and building your character is more about understanding the person you want to be. How can this make you more resilient? It gives you the ability to separate who you are from what you have been through. And that is huge.

# Contribution

There is power in being able to do something for others. Surprise a sick friend with chicken soup. Volunteer for a local organization. Make someone else happy so that you know that you can make a difference in not only your life, but others lives as well.

# Coping

Learn how to calm yourself down when it feels like all is lost. The past can haunt you if you let it. Look into deep breathing, progressive muscle relaxation, meditation, or mindfulness. You can do it. You just have to be brave enough to believe that you can.

# Control

Want to know what these other six Cs have in common? They are all ways to increase and improve your perception of control. Yes, sometimes things will be out of your control, especially when it comes to traumatic events. But that doesn't mean you can't control how a past trauma affects the rest of your life. And believing that is the key to believing that you can bounce back from what life throws at you—and start off in pursuit of your dreams!

*"A great book begins with an idea; a great life, with a determination."*

—Louis L'Amour,
*Education of a Wandering Man*

You must be vigilant in your determination, and immediately wipe out those negative feelings. They can start out small, and then it's easy to ignore them. A little twisting in your stomach, a twinge of anxiety in your brain, a pang in your heart. You shrug them off and seek a diversion. But if you leave them be, they will fester and multiply. Think of the weeds in your garden analogy. You must yank any negativity out by the roots!

---

## A NOTE FROM THE EXPERT: ALEXANDRA FARBENBLUM

I have spent the majority of my life surrounded by pregnant women. And yet, I can't seem to get pregnant.

My dad is a well-known obstetrician/gynecologist on the Upper East Side of Manhattan. I remember visiting the labor and delivery floor with my dad when I was thirteen years old. He was there doing his afternoon rounds, checking in with each of his patients who delivered the day or so before.

Dad's patients were still in a state of euphoric bliss, having just given birth. And I had the opportunity to run around with the man who made it all happen. One day, my dad came home to ask me if I wanted to see a delivery. He had a patient who was about to give birth to her fourth child— and I was about to see life being brought into the world.

Without even thinking about what this might entail, I eagerly accepted and ran with my dad to the hospital. Within moments, I found myself inches away from a patient who was painfully forcing herself to tolerate her contractions and bring forth this child. At one point, Dad asked me to hold the patient's leg back so the baby could have an easier exit point. Within seven minutes, the baby had come out, crying at the new world he had entered into.

And now, here I am at twenty-seven years old, happily married to the most incredible man, and I'm struggling to get pregnant—despite the many babies my father has brought into the world.

What happened to me? Why am I having trouble? Why can't the daughter of a doctor whose sole job is to bring new life into the world bring her own child in this world?

And isn't there such a thing as good juju?

When I was eighteen years old, I finally pushed my parents into explaining the large scar that was below my stomach flap (or fat). You know, the one where you go to the wax place and they ask you what your kids' names are because you have what appears to be a c-section scar?

I guess at some point I just assumed that it was normal to have a scar like that? Or that because I carried a few extra pounds it was natural to have a "dent" in your stomach—you know the line that happens when you sit in a weird position and your stomach just creases naturally? I also trusted my parents to tell me if something was wrong with me.

(I should probably also mention that I was a fully developed teenager without a period and no one had offered me the answers to explain why, where, or when. But, oddly, I hadn't worked up the nerve to ask any questions, either.)

My parents nonchalantly—with the same kind of casual tone you would use when you tell someone your name—explained that when I was three years old, I complained about a terrible pain in my side.

They took me to the doctor and were notified that I had an enlarged cyst on my left ovary and it needed to be removed. Immediately.

My left ovary was removed and was sewn up by the best plastic surgeon. I was left with only one ovary at the age of three. Luckily, my cyst was benign and I went on with my exciting kid life, doing kid things. I guess they just figured they would tell me…eventually?

And as the explanation of my secret scar was exposed, my parents also decided to explain the reason why I still hadn't gotten my period: I suffered from polycystic ovaries (PCOS). PCOS causes a woman to have infrequent menstrual periods and/or an excess of male hormones, which causes super annoying things like hair growth (thankfully, I didn't have it too bad). PCOS also means that I am prone to ovarian cysts.

The reason I hadn't gotten a period yet was because my body had been producing an excess of hormones. And the cyst that resulted in the removal of my ovary was also caused my body's hormonal imbalance.

It was a lot of information to take in all at once, but no one was worried. Everyone was pretty calm. My mom even reminded me that no one in our family had ever had trouble getting pregnant. The assumption was that of course there was no reason for me to have trouble when the time came.

Looking back now, I just have to laugh. Having trouble is an understatement. About a year or so after we got married, my husband and I started figuring out our next life steps. We began to look for a home for our future family and trying to conceive.

At first, the thought of "trying" was super-fun, even if we didn't succeed. But after a few months, my father suggested that we check in with a reproductive endocrinologist. Usually, couples are advised to wait until they have been trying for a minimum time period of six months to a year, but because of my history and my father's profession, we opted to meet with a specialist sooner.

And we are both really glad that we did.

We did some blood work and an expanded genetic breakdown and found that my husband and I are carriers for the same genetic mutation. Therefore, if we got pregnant, our child would have a high likelihood of becoming afflicted with it. Not only was the gene mutation an issue, but my PCOS was also affecting my chances of conceiving.

Armed with the harsh realities of all that we were dealing with, we decided that in vitro fertilization (IVF) was the only way to get pregnant with a healthy baby. During the IVF process, the lab needs saliva samples from the couple, as well as both sets of parents, to create a markup of what the embryo should not have.

Think of it as that mixing colors chart you learned in sixth grade art class. If our painting had green in it, it had our genetic mutation and that deemed our embryo unusable. So, after a few grueling weeks of waiting for the lab to create the test, we were finally given the go-ahead to begin injections.

The purpose of the injections is to trick your body into growing more than one follicle at a time. A follicle releases one egg every month, and that is how you ovulate. Your body only knows to release one egg every month, so it is essentially working in overdrive to grow many follicles at once.

As an FYI, here is a schedule of what happens on a day-to-day basis of an IVF patient (which lasts about twelve or so days):

*Good Morning!*

*Start your day by getting probed to assess the progress of your follicle development. Then get stabbed by a needle for daily blood work!*

*Bonus: As you get closer to your retrieval date, it gets more and more uncomfortable!*

*Time For Lunch!*

*Around lunchtime, you (anxiously) wait for a call from a doctor or nurse to tell you if your follicles are growing at the speed they need to be.*

*Good Night, Moon. Good Night, More Medication.*

*Before bed you must inject yourself with two different types of medications—both of which have the potential to make you into a full-blown crazy person!*

In my case, I also spent a considerable amount of time every evening praying to God that my ovary would survive this burden long enough to make it to my retrieval date.

After twelve days, it was finally Retrieval Day! I dressed myself in the stiffly starched hospital garb and was sedated in order for my eggs to be removed.

On my retrieval day, I had twenty-five eggs removed. (That's kind of a great number for a girl with one ovary.) Later that day, my eggs danced around with my husband's sperm in an attempt at fertilization. We had to wait about twenty-four hours to find out which of these mates hit the jackpot and awaited the number of how many fertilized—meaning which eggs were mature enough, because sometimes they just aren't ready to become adults.

The day after my retrieval, we were told that eleven embryos were fertilized. Before the week was over, we were down to five. The five fertilized eggs were biopsied and sent to the lab for a super-fancy check to see if my possible-petri-dish kids had our genetic disorder.

Since life is always full of surprises and adventures, the timing worked in such a way that while I was on my IVF journey, my husband and I moved into our forever home. The week we moved in was the same week as my egg retrieval, after which I was instructed to take it easy, relax, and not overstress myself.

I followed doctor's orders and tried to maintain some sort of calm in my life by feverishly unpacking as many boxes as I could. I was trying to feel more settled in my new home and to distract myself from waiting for the results of my potential petri-children.

There aren't enough boxes in the world to occupy your time as you wait for that call. IVF consumes you and your everyday life—not only with the daily updates from your doctor or nurse but also the calls from well-meaning friends and family members asking for updates. The waiting is grueling, and all I wanted was a kid, which is kinda what we were made to do. So how can it be so hard?

After eighteen days, my husband and I were told that all five embryos that were biopsied were deemed either "abnormal" or were marred by our genetic disorder.

Now, how shitty is that? I mean, you go through what feels like forever with the appointments, the testing, the blood work… and nothing is usable? What is wrong with me? Why do I deserve this? Is it the evil eye tormenting me? It's such a stroke of terrible luck, and the only thing you can naturally do is blame yourself.

After all the sadness, my husband and I decided to just keep swimming. We are now currently in the middle of our second round of IVF.

I can't lie, I am feeling so many different emotions. I am sad, scared, nervous, but most of all, I am hopeful. I am hopeful because there could only be good from here on out—at least, that's my hope. I wouldn't wish what my husband and I have gone through on our worst enemy. It is really hard and sad that something as easy (for other people) as getting pregnant should come this hard and sad for me.

This time, I know what to expect and how to react. I know that I will be a hormonal mess (again) and that it will be okay. I know that I have a husband who loves me and called me a "Freaking Gangster" for getting through all of my shots. You feel like a rock star when you go through IVF. You feel like you can conquer the world.

So, am I sad? Yeah, I'm sad. But I'm ready. I'm ready conquer this round and find those few perfect embryos. It will be nice to finally have some little Farbenblum's running around.

*Alexandra Farbenblum is a former communications director for a New York State Senator. She previously worked at Dan Klores Communications. She lives with her husband Michael in Woodmere, New York.*

---

## A NOTE FROM THE EXPERT: SHARONE SAPIR

As a nutritionist, most people find me because they want to lose weight. Nearly all of my clients think that they will be happier if they do. As you're reading this, you're probably nodding your head, thinking, "Hell, yeah I'll be happier if I lose weight."

And you know what? There's a good chance that you will be.

If you are overweight now and that is causing health problems, losing weight will help that.

If you don't feel comfortable in your clothes, and you feel self-conscious, then yeah, losing weight will help.

So, yeah, losing weight will make you happy-*er*. But happy?

Nope.

You are still going to struggle with finding that happiness. Because deep-seated happiness doesn't come from looking like a babe in your skinny jeans or pulling your belt four notches tighter.

Sorry.

Want to be happy with who you are for real?

***Accept responsibility for your role in your current body and your current situation.***

This first one is really hard. It's probably the hardest. Your ego doesn't easily allow you to admit when you've fucked up. It's always someone else's fault, isn't it? Even in regard to your weight.

*"Sally keeps bringing chocolate chip cookies to the office."*

*"I had a hard day, I can eat the whole pizza if I want to; I deserve it."*

*"This is the only me time I have, I'm going to enjoy it and eat however much I want."*

*"Calories shmalories. Since I blew it for the day, might as well stuff myself and start fresh tomorrow. Promise I'll be good."*

If you've ever said that last one, you need to find me on Instagram now so I can reprogram your brain (@sapirnutrition, *wink wink*).

The great thing about taking responsibility and truly owning it is that you are no longer the victim. And that's bad-ass. Because when you're a victim, things happen *to* you. There's no control.

But that's bullshit. And kinda insulting. Because so much in life is in your control. But to actually take that control, you have to admit when you fuck up. And that means growing up.

Every day, try to identify a time when your actions have led to an unfavorable outcome, either for you or for someone else. We get to exercise our free will every time we interact with someone else. Interactions are opportunities for us to make decisions that either better us or worsen us. When our intention is good, we often make good decisions. When our intentions stem from our ego—fear and arrogance—we often don't make good decisions. Getting into a habit of self-reflection will help alter your future actions in a positive way.

### *Be grateful for what you already have.*

I'm sure it's been forced down your throat by every self-help book, but hear me out.

More than thirty-five percent of the world does not have access to clean water. Have access to clean water? That's a win! And do you realizes that your chances of having been born are really, really, really small. One estimate is one in 400 trillion. You will never be happy if you don't appreciate the small things, which happen to be not so small.

Wherever you look, there's someone who has it better than you. More money, better hair, better body, smarter children, hotter spouse. And if there isn't, all you have to do is stare at the TV or social media and they will appear in .2 seconds.

Stop looking and comparing—you're wasting precious time!

Gratitude for what you already have will shift your perspective. It will help you stop feeling sorry for yourself, and it will help you be happy.

### *Be kind. Be kind to yourself, and be kind to others.*

Ever heard the term, kindness is contagious? Until I learned to drive, I always thought the term sounded hokie. But when I first started driving, I surprised myself by what an asshole driver I was, especially considering that I'm a pretty nice person. But over time, I realized that when someone was overtly kind, like letting me pass even though they had right of way, I was more inclined to do the same for someone else. And I am, dare I say, a nicer driver these days.

Because being on the receiving end of kindness feels good. And being kind feels good. So kindness actually is contagious. I would like to think that is because kindness taps into the source of the universe, which is love. Kindness feels right because it *is* right, and it's vital for our consciousness to evolve.

I know that's some deep shit. If you're interested in learning more, there are some great books out there. (One of my favorites is *My Big Toe* by Tom Campbell).

In the mean time, vow to do something nice for someone else every day, like holding a door, asking—and caring—about how they're feeling, or giving a genuine compliment.

### *Choose the right friends.*

The truth is, you're kinda stuck with family, and there's not much you can do if somebody is a crazy pants or a constant Debbie Downer. And the same goes for your co-workers.

But we live in an age where if you have access to the internet, you have access to new friends—and you can choose to have positive friends, even if you live in a town of negative people. It can be as easy as joining a supportive Facebook group based on your interests. Sure, the Miserables troll online, but I'm not kidding when I say there are thousands of online groups that weed out those people and preserve a safe, loving community. Your Granny didn't have access to that, but you do! So take advantage of what is out there.

You may not need all your friends. The one who constantly bitches about how unfair the world is? Can't find something nice to say about anyone? Makes little passive aggressive jabs at you? Leave him or her on the plate. Don't get dragged down.

### *Don't give up on your fitness goals.*

Start small.

If you want to lose weight, pick one healthy habit to adapt. Just one at a time. Success is built on habits, lots of small changes that accumulate.

Here are a few suggestions:

1. Drink a cup of water before every meal. Drinking water before a meal helps you feel fuller from that meal. If you do it consistently, you will eventually cut down on how many calories you eat, and that will *eventually* (key word here!) result in weight loss. Look at you! Here you are drinking water and being kinder!

2. Pick one meal a day and add a serving of vegetables. Vegetables help you feel full on few calories, and when you habitually add them to your meals, they displace other foods that are higher in calories. Doing this every day will help to cut down on the number of calories you take in, and will *eventually* (key word! key word!) result in weight loss.

3. Leave some food on your plate. This is another way to simply cut down on how much you're eating. Which we know results in weight loss. If you're always leaving ten percent of the food on your plate, you're cutting down on your food intake by ten percent, and that will *eventually* (ding! ding! ding!) lead to weight loss.

Changing anything in your life is hard. That's why weight loss is so difficult for just about everyone. It involves making many sustainable changes, and it takes a very long time to see the results.

But what most people get wrong is that they think changes have to be big, that small changes don't count. I highly recommend the book *Atomic Habits*, by James Clear, if you want to fully understand how very small changes when done consistently lead to very big outcomes.

It applies to everything. Break it all down into baby steps and focus on one tiny change at a time. You can be happy.

*Sharone Sapir is a nutritionist with a private practice in Long Island, New York. Sharone completed her Masters of Science in nutrition and education from Columbia University, and she loves using inappropriate humor to get her point across on her Instagram account, @sapirnutrition. Her tell-it-like-it-is attitude isn't for the faint of heart, but if you like honesty, don't hesitate to reach out: sharonesapir.com.*

"*Remember your dreams and fight for them.
You must know what you want from life.*"

—Paulo Coelho

Paulo Coelho certainly had to fight for his dreams. As a teenager, he knew what he wanted from life: to be a writer. When he told his mother, she said: "My dear, your father is an engineer. He's a logical, reasonable man with a very clear vision of the world. Do you actually know what it means to be a writer?" (Unfortunately, no one really does—because they don't teach it as a viable career choice.)

Still, Paulo insisted. He became introverted—a natural and, I think, healthy defense from unrelenting opposition—and refused to follow a traditional path. So his parents committed him to a mental institution when he was seventeen. He escaped from it three times and was finally released at age twenty.

Paulo is the author of the phenomenally successful international bestseller *The Alchemist*, as well as other books that have touched countless lives. If he had succumbed to the pressure of a "traditional" path, not only would he have lost his own dreams, but he would also have not produced the works that have affected so many others.

The arts and sciences are fraught with stories of people who faced stunning adversity and still persisted.

## Concrete Action

# Head full steam toward your dreams

1. Go back over your journal entries and notes on why this journey is so important to you.

2. Speak with other people who are on a similar path. Socialize with them!

3. Speak with people who have already reached this (or a similar) goal. Seek mentorship, or at least encouragement. Ask about their pitfalls and how they pulled themselves out of them. Everyone has had pitfalls, and learning how others have made it is inspirational and motivational. If you can't locate someone in person, reach out on the internet or through social media. Or, if you can't connect to anyone, read about people's stories of reaching success.

4.  Every day, devote time to your passion. Even if you only have five minutes. You must train your mind and soul: You don't just *want* to do this, you *are* doing this! It's not in the future—it's *now*!

*"You simply have to put one foot in front of the other and keep going. Put blinders on and plow right ahead."*

—George Lucas

*Star Wars* would never have been made if not for George's blind persistence. Movie executives didn't think it would find an audience!

There will be hard days—even at the end. Especially at the end. (That's why they have that saying, "It's always darkest before the dawn" even though it's not true—dark is dark.) There will be days of rejection. If you start to doubt yourself, I urge you to go back to these actions!

*"Fall seven times, stand up eight."*

—Chinese Proverb

If you are lucky enough to already be living your dreams, you must still protect and nurture your passion.

*"Lose your dreams and you might lose your mind."*

—Mick Jagger

Already living your dreams? There are still **concrete actions** to undertake.

1.  Surround yourself with like-minded people (see Step Three).
2.  Continually seek knowledge and growth in your passion. Read the latest articles and books about it or things having to do with it, have discussions with your like-minded friends, go to gatherings such as conventions, celebrations, or any events.

3. Be thankful each day for the privilege of doing what you love. You may manifest this in any way you feel comfortable, at any lengths that feel right to you.

## STEP EIGHT
# CELEBRATE YOURSELF

*"I celebrate myself, and sing myself."*

—Walt Whitman,
"Song of Myself"

You are unique. There is no other you! You are like a snowflake, but better because you won't melt.

And yet, from childhood, people have tried to make you into someone else. From friendships and peer pressure to teachers to parents. Sometimes this was done innocently and with the best of intentions; sometimes it was done with malice.

It wasn't fair for you to face such challenge at a young age. How could you be expected to stay true to your unique self before you understood what was going on?

*"The hardest challenge is to be yourself in a world where everyone is trying to make you be somebody else."*

—E. E. Cummings

*"To be yourself in a world that is constantly trying to make you something else is the greatest accomplishment."*

—Ralph Waldo Emerson

But now, you know.

You are a gift. To the universe. To others. But above all, to yourself.

*It's time to accept this gift of yourself.*

When you embrace yourself—your true, beautiful self—with no judgments and only love, you will feel the happiness welling in your heart.

What do I mean by "celebrate yourself"? Well, what do you think I mean? There's no wrong way. You can do it by posting cool things about your life on social media, or on a blog. You can call relatives or old friends. You can chat with people at work about what you're up to, or what you've learned or accomplished. You can go buy yourself a sharp new outfit or a fancy cup of coffee. Or, you can whisper to the universe: "I love myself."

At first this may feel awkward, painful, or even impossible. You don't want to do these things. Perhaps the loving yourself part seems the hardest.

The more you celebrate yourself, the easier it becomes.

And if you don't celebrate yourself, how can you expect the universe to celebrate you?

*"With our thoughts we make the world."*

—Buddha

This is not some gobbledygook. This is the law of attraction—used over the centuries to achieve goals. Celebration begets celebration. And a celebration is always happy! (More on the law of attraction later.)

Celebrating yourself is also about honoring yourself. Acknowledge how far you've come. Tell yourself just how proud you are. I often say "Good job!" to myself after I complete a task even as seemingly meaningless as cleaning the floor. It's not meaningless! Nothing you accomplish is meaningless! Remember I mentioned breaking up tasks into small pieces? If you break up accomplishments the same way, you'll always have something to celebrate. Your vibes will carry you and lift you up so that you feel like a champ while you're cleaning your toilet! (And you are!)

---

## A NOTE FROM THE EXPERT: ALEXA CARLIN

*"Whatever the mind can conceive and believe, it can achieve."*

—Napoleon Hill

I have always been a fan of the law of attraction, the understanding that if you think positively and visualize the outcome you desire, you'll have a better chance attracting that outcome into your life. But let's face it, we can't always be positive. When we experience tragedy, death, failure, illness, or poverty, it's very hard to immediately look at the situation in a positive light. It takes time to overcome those negative feelings, sometimes years.

However, what if I told you that you can heal your life with your thoughts. Would you believe me?

Senior year of college my life changed forever. I was at the University of Florida when I was rushed to the emergency room. My body went into septic shock. I was quickly induced into a medical coma and was given a one percent chance of living. The doctors told my mom, "Call your family, she has twenty-four hours to live."

I was in the coma for six days, and when I woke up out of the coma in the ICU, I had a mask on my face, a tube down my throat, and I was hooked up to nine different bags of antibiotics. I couldn't move, breathe, or speak on my own. I couldn't even have a glass of water. All I had was my mind.

During this time, I pictured my mind to be this pure healthy pink color, while the rest of my body was black and rotting away. I would push down this pink color to try healing my body. I would push with every ounce of energy I had left. A few days later, I was discharged from the hospital and on to a full recovery.

The doctors believed it was a miracle. I *knew* it was a miracle, but a miracle I created.

We all have this limitless power. A power so strong that it is incomprehensible, yet when tapped into, you know exactly how to use it. When the mind is healthy, you have the world at your fingertips. You can create any life you want, have anything you desire, and live freely and happily. You know how people say, *happiness is a choice*? Well, they are exactly right. Happiness is a choice. Health is a choice.

You can choose to let life's circumstances inhibit you from fulfilling your potential, or you can heal your life with the power of your thoughts.

It's simple. If you are in a dark place in your life, find the light. When you are living in the light, be present.

So how do you find the light? Choose light. See light. Feel light.

When I was in the coma, I pictured the light. I was a free soul running with the wind. I was not in a body; I was a being of light. I had a willingness to survive.

When I was out of the coma, I was in so much pain. Suffering like you couldn't even imagine. So the only way to overcome this pain and survive was to visualize the end result. The end result was water for me. I pictured something tangible. All I wanted was a glass of water. I pictured myself running on a high school track. I was running and running and when I reached the end I had all my loved ones around me throwing a *huge* glass of ice-cold water on me and into my mouth.

My thoughts during this time were, "water at the end of the race; water at the end of the race; water at the end of the race." I continued to say it over and over in my head and I pictured the end result. Picturing the light at the end of the tunnel helped me tune out my thoughts of darkness: the pain and the suffering.

This technique can be used in any area of your life. If you've been dumped, got fired, are suffering from chronic illness, or lost all your money by making a wrong decision, picture the end result you desire. Make your mind healthy so you can heal the rest of your life. Picture the light.

Ask yourself:
*What does the light look like for me?*
*What does being in the light feel like?*
*If I were living in the light, what would I do?*

The answers that arise are the solutions to your problems. The answers will guide you toward healing your life and creating the present you desire to live in.

Change your thoughts, and you can change your life.

It all starts with healing your mind by allowing your positive thoughts to stay with you and your negative thoughts to flee. If you continue to perceive your situation negatively, you will never be able to move forward. Spread positive thoughts into every area of your life that is wrong right now and visualize the end result. Do this every single day, multiple times a day, and sooner than you think, you'll be living a life full of light.

*At seventeen, Alexa Carlin was a CEO. At twenty-one, doctors gave her a one percent chance to live. Alexa is a serial entrepreneur and a nationally renowned public speaker sharing her story and experiences authentically to audiences all over the world. She launched the Women Empower X (WEX) in 2016 and it became the largest event for female entrepreneurs and change leaders in South Florida and Washington D.C. within its first year and is now growing to a third city in 2019. Alexa's mission is to make a difference in at least one person's life every single day. For more information, please visit https://www.alexacarlin.com/and https://womenempowerx.com/*

## Scientifically Speaking

On a scientific note, celebrating small victories is a way of producing dopamine—a neurotransmitter that motivates you to work for your goals. Scientific study shows that recognizing each step along the way keeps your dopamine flow steady, so you can keep going.

Why do you think I divided your journey in this book into ten steps? If I dumped it all on you at once, or if I expected you to hang on until the end without any break or acknowledgement of your accomplishments along the way, you'd very likely give up!

If you keep putting off the celebration you may never get to it—because you've experienced no positive reinforcement. Not only is it sad to deny yourself the pleasure of an acknowledgement—you may be metaphorically shooting yourself in the foot, sabotaging yourself from going any further. It is important to actually celebrate, whether you pick yourself a flower, write yourself a note, buy yourself a bottle of wine, or treat yourself to a nice meal.

If you wait until a big victory and actually make it—it could be your last one, at least for a while. You may crash after that dopamine high you've been chasing.

It's also crucial to have the next small goal set before you celebrate. You must keep your momentum going!

---

## A NOTE FROM THE EXPERT: ELORA PHILBRICK

Emotional Freedom Technique, also known as Emotional Functional Tapping (EFT), is used to reduce stress, depression, tension, and anxiety. EFT is similar to acupuncture in that it is believed to rebalance the body's internal energy source by applying pressure to surfaces of the body to relieve pain or tension.

If the idea of tapping on your body in order to change your emotions sounds totally crazy, it really shouldn't.

It's a lot like getting a massage, except that EFT requires pressure through the fingertips, and you can easily do it yourself. Tapping your body with your fingertips is thought to stimulate your meridian points, the places in your body where your source of energy is thought to flow. In traditional Chinese medicine this energy is referred to as *chi*.

So where do you tap, and when?

Your body has numerous acupoints, for example at your temples, between collarbones, and at the top of your sternum. Each acupoint serves to heal specific individual functions depending on where the pressure is applied.

These acupoints are thought to aid in not only mental health, but physical health as well. Tapping on the pressure points can relieve ailments such as indigestion, headaches, cramps, and even seasonal colds. Tapping on the indentation between the big toe and second toe on the top of the foot is believed to relieve stress. Tapping directly below the lower edge of your kneecap can revitalize your *chi* and increase energy levels.

So next time you are feeling anxious, depressed, tense, or stressed—whether it's at home or at work—give it a try. Many people claim they have used these tapping techniques to realign, re-center, and regain composure.

*Elora Philbrick is a graduate of Franklin Pierce University and received her BA in English and mass communications. She has been published in* An Anthology of Emerging Poets 2017 *by Z Publishing House and was awarded the Harriet Wilson Fiction Prize in 2016. Elora has experience in writing, editing, publishing, journalism reporting, and investigative journalism. Currently, she resides in New Hampshire and can be contacted at* ephilbrick96@gmail.com.

## Concrete Action

# Celebrate yourself

*"You yourself, as much as anybody in the entire universe, deserve your love and affection."*

—Buddha

1. You just learned more about Emotional Freedom Technique. I discovered it through a class at The Learning Annex—actually an extra class I threw in because it was buy two get one free. This turned out to be one of the most important choices in my life. I felt freer and lighter that very night—and good things started happening in me and for me in the days and weeks after. A revelation!

*"Your task is not to seek for love, but merely to seek and find all the barriers within yourself that you have built against it."*

—Rumi

2. Meditation and/or breathing is a great way of celebrating yourself by allowing for reflection, clarity, and—literally—room to breathe! My breathing used to be gasping and desperate; I didn't even realize this until it was pointed out to me. When I started concentrating on my breathing, slowing down and deepening my breaths, I noticed a remarkable change. I began to see my possibilities from a whole new perspective. A wide view was opened up. It was like freeing myself from a prison.

*"I know but one freedom and that is the freedom of the mind."*

—Antoine de Saint-Exupéry

Later, I learned Transcendental Meditation. That, too, is a remarkable way to honor myself by blocking out twenty minutes twice a day devoted to clearing my mind. These days, there are meditation apps, and of course there's always YouTube. There are many ways to meditate. Try it!

*"The thing about meditation is: You become more and more you."*

—David Lynch

3. Yoga is not my thing. But maybe it will be yours! My older son Michael loves it and absolutely uses it to celebrate himself.

*"Yoga is not about touching your toes. It is what you learn on the way down."*

—Jigar Gor

4. Exercise is a way to honor your body. That means you are celebrating yourself and (as mentioned earlier) also getting those endorphins going! You will feel uplifted and empowered when you exercise, in any way you enjoy it.

5. Spell out your successes! When you were in school you wrote reports about awesome people. Write one about yourself! What's the title? You can also write a poem about yourself. Or an article/blog post. If you were tweeting about yourself, what would you say?

6. Look at your baby pictures! Who doesn't love a cute baby? Looking at baby pictures of yourself reminds you of that joyous spirit you were as a baby, when the world was your oyster. And no matter what you've been through, that happy spirit is still inside you, at your core. Celebrate your spirit by displaying these pictures where you'll see them frequently, and say hello to the little you as you pass by them.

Make sure you make time for something special to honor and celebrate yourself each day—even if it's just quiet time with coffee, reflecting. Think about how much you love being you and how proud of yourself you are!

# STEP NINE

# SPREAD JOY

*"You are the universe unfolding."*

—Zen saying

You are a product of the environment you create. So why wouldn't you spread joy?

The vibes you put out are the ones that return to you—like a boomerang. This is why they say, "You get what you give."

But it's more than a boomerang—it's a multiplying of joy. Because when you bring more joy in others, they will send more joy out as well—and it keeps expanding.

This also relates to the law of attraction. But what *is* the law of attraction? The basic concept is that whatever you think of, you attract into your life. This is a concept that has been around for centuries—proof of which are many quotes by Buddha and ancient philosophers. This book is not about the law of attraction (there are many books about it—most famously *The Secret*, which I list in "further reading") and you can decide for yourself whether you put belief in it or want to try and use it, but I think you should be conscious of its possibilities. When you spread joy, take note of the response you get. I'll bet you start finding yourself surrounded by more joyful people.

If you're spreading joy, happy people want to be around you!

*"Joy is a net of love by which you can catch souls."*

—Mother Teresa

The other great thing about spreading joy is that when you do this, you are also manifesting joy within yourself—you can't give away what you don't have. And so you become a "joy generator."

*"Spread love everywhere you go. Let no one ever come to you without leaving happier."*

—Mother Teresa

So how do you spread joy? This is probably the easiest step, because there are so many ways. They're simple, and the more you do, the more you want to do, and the happier you feel. This is a step you will continue for the rest of your life—and you'll be happy to do it!

The hardest part may be beginning. Hopefully you've been doing these steps and are feeling better—but maybe you aren't. Maybe you wake up and face the day with your head caved in (a line from The Police song "Invisible Sun," which I've always thought is such a great description for sadness and depression). If this is so, and you aren't under the care of a doctor or social worker, I ask you to please make an appointment. If you are clinically depressed, our steps cannot work on their own. You need help. There are clinics available if you can't afford a private practice. I also recommend Chinese medicine—but again, you need to go to the appropriate doctor to get the proper herbs. Don't order them randomly on Amazon or eBay!

Professional treatment aside, if you wake up sad in the morning, the first person you need to spread joy to is yourself. You can do this in many ways!

## FROM THE DOCTOR'S DESK: LINDSAY S. WEISNER, PSYD

Have you ever tried to quit something? To let go of someone or something that is holding you back? Like carbs or sugar? Or maybe it's something bigger, like smoking, or alcohol, or that crappy bad boy ex-boyfriend you swore you would never go back to?

And I know; I get it. You're a planner. A thinker. And so, you prep for quitting your *something* like it's a fitness resolution for your wedding day. (A fitness resolution you will stick to this time, because you know full well how expensive those wedding photos are, and you do not want to spend the rest of the marriage looking at your wedding photos and focusing on your back fat instead of your smile.)

You will no longer walk by that overpriced-and-totally-worth-it bakery on your way to work. That's temptation, and you are prepped to avoid that crap. Halloween candy from nine months ago—gone. It's stale, but it's still sugar, and who knows how desperate you could get after a few days of black coffee.

You've got your Nicorette gum and your sparkling water, and your friends have been thoroughly briefed about what to do if you start talking about how much you miss the same guy you previously declared the world's biggest asshat.

And then… life happens. Because it always does.

Your boss is too critical. Your kids don't appreciate you. (Welcome to parenthood!)

Or maybe it's your birthday or you had a crap day or your college boyfriend got engaged to a woman who dresses like she walked out of a Laura Ashley catalog and her taste in China patterns is regretful. (At best.)

Where are you then? Where is your strength and fortitude and will power and—most importantly, what happened to your desire to change?

I live in a small town. Small enough that I regularly run into my patients at the grocery store, the pharmacy, and when I'm picking up my children from school.

A few weeks ago, I pulled into the school parking lot to drop off my children. And at the same moment my son opened the car door, a large SUV—moving much faster than I was comfortable with given my son's proximity (although probably not as fast as I envisioned in this midst of my massive anxiety)—pulled in next to us and *honked*. This woman honked at my kid, who she almost ran over. She honked at my kid to get out of her way.

And when she pulled in next to me and I reassured myself that my son was safe, I realized that I knew her. Not particularly well, but I knew her name (not her actual real name, of course) was Barbara, and I knew that Barbara had always been lovely to me. I also knew that Barbara was a single parent to three young kids, and her father had recently been diagnosed with cancer, and she clearly had a tremendous amount on her plate. And yet, I wanted to scream many, many, many expletives that would not have been taken well, considering the fact that we were both standing on school grounds.

If I yelled at her, she would have no doubt yelled back. I mean, wouldn't you yell at someone who was yelling at you? Right, wrong, or indifferent, we all go into a fight or flight survival mode when someone is yelling at us. Especially if adrenaline is sky-high as the result of a near-car accident… or the near-maiming or murder of my kid. I'm fairly sure Barbara was pretty damn hyped up, too, since she had almost just run over my kid. (Yeah, her honking at my kid pissed me off, like, a lot, but in the heat of the moment, people do weird things.)

I didn't yell. I kinda didn't see the point.

My yelling wouldn't have made my heart stop beating out of my chest, and it wouldn't have quelled the massive wave of panic and worst-case-scenario thinking that was threatening to drown me. In fact, yelling at Barbara would have amped up all my physiological symptoms of stress (increase in heart beat and blood pressure, change in respiration, increase in perspiration) and made me feel even more angry and upset. (I like to envision me as the Incredible Hulk in this scenario of what could have been.)

So I didn't yell. But I wanted to. It was that damn honk. It stuck with me in the moment, and it was still there, nine hours later, when I was proudly telling my husband (i.e. bragging) about how well I handled it.

"But can you believe she honked at the kid she almost hit? I mean, she almost hit him and she has the nerve to—"

"Eh, people do strange things in scary moments," my brilliant husband reminded me.

Which is true. But that honk still pissed me off.

Still, I didn't yell at Barbara when she honked. And since I didn't yell, Barbara wasn't put in a position where it would have been natural to get defensive, and so Barbara didn't have to yell back. The day didn't end in anger and embarrassment for either of us, or our children who would have been totally mortified.

Let's go back to what Barbara did, what her action was in this scenario. Her action was careless. She may have been distracted by concern for her father or a text on her phone or an argument her kids were having about who got to eat the last bag of mini-muffins.

Or maybe she just made a mistake.

It happens.

And there is absolutely nothing I can do about her actions, about what she did. The only thing I can do—and the only thing I did do—was focus on my reaction. In this case, I changed my reaction from anger and outrage to compassion.

I'm proud of how I handled the situation in the moment.

Psychologists have long spoken about something called the Fundamental Attribution Bias. Simply put, this is the tendency to blame others when things go wrong, coupled with the tendency to expect that others should not blame you.

For example, if the waitress forgets to bring you french fries and messes up your drink order, it's because she is a crappy waitress. But if I forget to stop at the store for bread because I have *literally* had the day from hell, it's obviously not my fault. I just had a really bad day. The shorthand is essentially, "You're an asshole; I'm just having a bad day."

What if we could give other people the benefit of the doubt when they mess up, the same way that we (subconsciously) give ourselves the benefit of a doubt when we do something wrong?

Not to toot my own horn (as I totally toot my own horn) but that's kinda what I did when I opted not to yell at Barbara and her stupid, annoying, self-righteous honk. I put myself in her shoes and cut her some slack.

Anger isn't my *something* that I need to get rid of. And trust me, there are plenty of times that I react without thinking things through then a short while later, with my tail between my legs, I apologize for my actions. Or my words. Or my decisions, which could have been better.

So, let's get back to you for a moment. What's that *something* you are trying to leave behind? And how would things be different if you focused on your reactions?

I suppose you can rid your house of everything with sugar, or reroute your path to work in a way that avoids every bakery, donut shop, and pizzeria from home to office, but eventually you're gonna come across a bread basket. And sure, that bread basket is totally manageable when all is well in the world, but what happens that day when everything goes wrong?

Do you cave in to carb heaven and just blame it on your boss? Grab a cigarette or loot through your old phone bills for your crappy ex-boyfriend's phone number? Pour yourself a nice, stiff drink?

Or do you take a step back in that moment and adjust your reaction? Because your reaction is kinda key to everything.

Do you give in to that bread basket and slap the blame on a stressful day?

You can. But you don't have to. And maybe you shouldn't, because you're better than that.

It is your reaction that is important. Not the action of your boyfriend leaving his shoes in the middle of the bedroom room floor for the forti-eth time.

A funny thing about that near-death (at least in my mind) experience I had with Barbara in the elementary school parking lot: A few days after this occurred, I was in session with a patient of mine, who has struggled her entire life with issues of anger.

Lilly is beautiful and bright, and she Moms the pants off of most women I know. But, I swear, she came out of the womb with her fists up, ready to (verbally) fight off the injustices and slights she perceives in the world.

Yeah, she's a badass bitch. But she's really unhappy with the anger she feels toward everyone, about everything, (almost) all the time.

Her oppositional behavior leaves her feeling lonely. She often feels like she has no friends, and she frequently sees slights where none were intended, and snubs that may have been mere coincidence.

"Oh my god," Lilly announced at the start of our session, "I could not believe that woman almost ran over your child!"

I laughed.

"Were you there, or did you hear about it?" I asked.

(Like I said, it's a small town.)

"I was right there! I honked to try to get her to stop, because I saw your son and she definitely did not!"

"Wait, you honked?" I asked in confusion. (And amazement, because what are the chances of this entire scenario taking place.)

"Of course I did!" Lilly said. "That woman was about to hit your kid, she didn't even see him! It was the only way I could think of to get her attention!"

The honk. That honk that I heard, that sound that really irritated me, the one thing about the whole event that filled me with a few moments of righteous indignation and that "How dare you!" feeling. That honk was from someone I couldn't even see at the moment, looking out for me and my son. That honk was not even close to how my mind originally interpreted it.

"I was so pissed, it's like she wasn't even looking!" Lilly continued. "You must have been furious! I'm just glad he is okay."

Life is really, really weird sometimes. And in my job, that I love so very much, this kind of weirdness, or synchronicity, abounds.

What if I had unleashed my fear and rage at Barbara because of her careless driving and her self-righteous honk? What if I had yelled and cursed and cried and made a scene because of what she did? Or in this case, what I *thought* she did? It would have been… awkward at best.

And what are the chances that Lilly, a stellar mom who struggles with her own anger, is the person to bear witness to my decision to hold onto my own anger and fear—to hold onto my feelings and react in a way I could be proud of, instead of reacting in a way that would have felt really good in that moment?

So, I took the synchronicity and went with it. Because true change withstands pressure and time. And for Lilly, her children are her number one priority, and there would be no greater pressure to her than the idea of someone endangering her child. And as for time? This seemed like a perfect moment to start working with her a little differently.

"Hey, Lilly, have I told you my theory about action and reaction? I think it might be something for you to use, to help you let go of your anger."

*Names were changed to protect identities, but I swear to God this whole crazy story happened.*

---

## Concrete Action

# Awakening joy in yourself

1. Look in the mirror and smile. You can also wish yourself a good morning, and tell yourself how awesome you are!

2. Treat yourself to a nice breakfast you enjoy.

3. Drink from a special mug.

4. Watch the sunrise—it's nature's beautiful miracle!

*"It is during our darkest moments that we must focus to see the light."*

—Aristotle

We can literally watch the light come from the darkness each morning!

5. Cuddle with a pet. (Okay, this is actually the pet spreading joy to you, but you are taking the action to interact with it.) If it's a pet you can't actually cuddle, like a fish, you can nurture it.

6. Wear clothes you like and feel good in.

7. Devote some early morning moments to something you enjoy, like writing, reading, listening to music, or turning on your favorite talk show!

8. Avoid the news, if possible. It can wait! I would also recommend avoiding social media, unless you have specific feel-good places you feel you need to go. This is not only because it can be upsetting, but also mind-muddling.

*"Truth is ever to be found in simplicity, and not in the multiplicity and confusion of things."*

—Isaac Newton

As I mentioned earlier, the power of simplicity on our psyche is proven. It's like we're lifting a great weight from our minds. Social media is not simple, and I think a simple morning is a great way to spread joy to yourself—considering that once you leave the house, you can't control how simple your day is. This ties nicely with our next concrete action:

9. Mediate and/or do breathing exercises.

10. The night before, write yourself a good morning note and leave it by the coffee pot!

11. Another thing you can do the night before is get everything ready for the morning, like setting up the coffee pot. Then in the morning, you can thank yourself for the gift!

12. Create your own! After all, this is about spreading joy to yourself! What appeals to you?

Now that you're fired up, you can generate joy for others!

*"Sprinkle joy."*

—Ralph Waldo Emerson

This Emerson quote makes me think of two things: water sprinklers and sprinkles on cupcakes. Both provide happiness!

A great joy in a quote is in the way each person interprets it. When I share quotes, it's one way in which I spread joy!

*"I've learned that people will forget what you said, people will forget what you did, but people will never forget how you made them feel."*

—Maya Angelou

There are so many ways to spread joy, and you can think of specific ones to tailor for people you know. The concrete actions which follow are just starting points!

## Concrete Action

# Spreading joy

1.  Smile!

2.  Practice random acts of kindness.

*"Be kind whenever possible. It is always possible."*

—*Dalai Lama*

3.  Be supportive, positive, and encouraging.

4.  Congratulate.

5.  When on social media, take the time to "like" and "love" posts— and a comment means even more. This is our new way of expressing care and interacting, and people appreciate it.

6.  Make a point of greeting people you pass every day, encounter in stores, or work with.

7.  Write a note to someone you love—kids, partner, family, friends. You can scrawl it on a Post-it and stick it anywhere as a little surprise, put it in a lunch bag or in a notebook, or on a cell phone. You can also write it on a postcard and mail it! (A text or e-mail works, too—but there's something touching about a physical, hand-written gesture.)

8.  Give little gifts. They don't have to be expensive, just something to give a lift. They can be personalized for specific people or the same thing for everyone. I used to give out little bitty rubber chickens with a business card saying, "Love thy chicken as thyself." Then I added, "Selene Castrovilla's books are something to cluck about!"

with my website. So, it was promotional, but more importantly, it brought happiness to others. I never met a person who didn't want the gift of a little rubber chicken. I've also used "happy clams"—plastic clams with the card, "You'll be as happy as your clam reading Selene Castrovilla's books." Neither of these gifts have anything to do with what I write. My idea was to spread joy, and then people would want to know me. I also find that candy works well in any situation! (Except at the dentist?)

9. Suggest books that people might find enlightening—or at least engrossing.

10. Share funny and relatable anecdotes, in-person and on social media.

11. Post quotes you are affected by on social media.

The possibilities of spreading joy are endless—to those you know and to strangers as well.

## STEP TEN

# BE GRATEFUL FOR THIS MOMENT

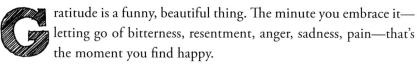ratitude is a funny, beautiful thing. The minute you embrace it— letting go of bitterness, resentment, anger, sadness, pain—that's the moment you find happy.

I know you've felt it in patches. You've grasped at it, like a child reaching for snowflakes. But like the snow, it's melted in your hands.

You think you need some special occasion to feel grateful. But gratitude is a state of mind. I saw a sign by a church that said:

**"Thanksgiving is thanks living."**

It's true. We don't need to segregate our thankfulness to a season or any reason. Our existence is enough.

*"If the only prayer you ever say in your entire life is thank you, it will be enough."*

—Meister Eckhart

You've been looking for happy. But just like Dorothy was searching for home and had the power to go there all along, you always had the power to be happy. It's not actually a destination—it's here. It's now. It's in every moment you've chosen to be happy, and every moment in the future you *choose* to be happy.

*"We do not remember days, we remember moments."*

—Cesare Pavese

Guess what? Those moments are your life.

*"Be happy for this moment. This moment is your life."*

—Omar Khayyam

---

## A NOTE FROM THE EXPERT: ERIN O'CALLAGHAN

I was thirty-two years old and enjoying life to the max. I was dancing every chance I could, eating out, traveling, and having fun exploring a new city with my husband.

And I had cancer.

Again.

The first time I was diagnosed, I was fifteen years old.

I had the first cancer from ages fifteen to sixteen—osteosarcoma. This is an aggressive bone cancer that spread from my right leg to my lungs. I had a thirty percent chance of survival and underwent many surgeries, plus fifteen months of aggressive chemotherapy to save my life.

It worked.

If I'm being honest with myself, during the sixteen years between the first diagnosis and the second, I always felt like I was living on borrowed time. I was excited and exuberant and trying to take advantage of everything life had to offer: music, concerts, nights out with friends. And lest you think it was all loud noise and fun times, I was also devoted to my schoolwork, my research, my students, and my patients. In between these two cancer diagnoses, I earned my PhD in clinical psychology, I moved around the country for my education and training, and I got married.

I received the call from my endocrinologist on June 17, 2009. One day after my thirty-second birthday.

Papillary thyroid cancer.

I was assured that my prognosis was excellent. I had a ninety-five percent chance of survival, and as opposed to the fifteen months of chemotherapy and multiple surgeries to treat the osteosarcoma, thyroid cancer was supposed to be a breeze. One surgery to remove my thyroid, a lifetime of taking Synthroid every day, and my life would be back to normal.

But this second diagnosis of cancer upended my world, despite the near perfect prognosis.

As a teenager, I struggled with the intense chemotherapy treatments and had numerous side effects that were grueling, exhausting, and just simply awful. But, I never doubted I would survive. At thirty-two, I had I earned my PhD and was completing a competitive postdoctoral-fellowship at the Children's Hospital of Los Angeles. I was married to my college sweetheart, living in West Hollywood, and enjoying the life I had always dreamed of. I certainly never thought I'd have cancer again. At least not until I was old and gray. That reality was okay with me—I was on borrowed time anyway.

But to be diagnosed with a *second* cancer by thirty-two? Who does this happen to? I did not then and still do not now know anyone who has had cancer twice—at any age. And yes, all of the cliché thoughts popped in my head: "Why me?" "I'm going to die." "This isn't fair."

These were all the same questions I had at age fifteen. But when I was fifteen, I wasn't scared of dying, or scared of anything at all. I just brushed my fears away and I told myself that I would never die young. I would beat this. And my family told me this, too. I was surrounded by boundless positivity, which was wonderful and life-saving. As a teenager, I benefitted from that adolescent egocentrism that I would later learn about in my child development classes.

I remember asking my oncologist to let me see Metallica and Guns N'

Roses at the Rose Bowl in October 1992. I had just finished my first round of chemo, and I was obsessed with Guns N' Roses. Axl's passion, lyrics, and piano-playing on "November Rain" were all an inspiration to me. I felt like I simply couldn't miss out on such a historical concert just because of cancer. After all, I was going to live through this, so why can't I just go sit with 60,000 fellow fans and enjoy this show?

My oncologist granted me permission to go to the concert after my bloodwork indicated that my immune system could most likely handle that kind of exposure to germs. I remember every minute of that concert. Everything was amplified. This was happiness.

At thirty-two years of age, with my life set up exactly the way I had always dreamed, I was not prepared to go through another diagnosis of cancer. But no one gave me a choice. And without the benefit of adolescent egocentrism, I was forced to face the possibility—albeit a tiny possibility this time—that I might die from this cancer.

This possibility shook me to the core, but it also gifted me with moments of pure joy. Kind of like Axl did all those years ago at the Rose Bowl.

I found that I appreciated and valued my husband, my dog, the sunny LA skies, food, and music more than I had before the diagnosis. I was an adult now and had the financial freedom to live a little more. We went to see live music more, ate out at delicious restaurants, and spent more time with family and friends. I also did simple things like watch birds, or listen to the traffic and wind and city noises. I was living in the moment—that elusive and much-desired frame of mind that so many try to achieve. I didn't have to read books or pay for expensive yoga classes to achieve this state. I was there because of the threat of death.

In July of 2012, I had a thyroidectomy. The surgery was more painful and involved than I expected. And I had been through many grueling and painful surgeries: limb salvage and revision to my right leg and two surgeries to remove tumors from my lungs, which left me in the ICU. I knew what pain and suffering was, and yet I was suffering after they removed my thyroid. I couldn't swallow and I couldn't breathe easily.

I actually felt sorry for myself, which was pretty unusual for me. After osteosarcoma, I was left with a permanent disability—I have limited mobility in my right knee and have to wear a plastic brace every day to walk.

However, I never (and still don't) let this stop me from doing what I wanted to do. I'm not talking about running a marathon or propelling myself down a mountain on skis. I know I can't physically do those things, and I accepted that long ago. I'm referring to not allowing the fact that I *had* cancer or *have* a disability stop me from feeling any differently about myself. I like who I am and how I look, and I know I'm bright and capable. I set goals (like earning my PhD), and I know I can achieve these goals.

So, I had never really felt sorry for myself before thyroid cancer. It was a foreign concept and one that thankfully didn't last long. But, I did let myself feel this sadness and loss for a bit of time during my experience with thyroid cancer. It *does* suck to have cancer (even the "good" ones); it *isn't* fair, and it *is* painful. It felt good to acknowledge and feel that this time around.

After the thyroidectomy, it took several weeks before I started to feel better. A month post-surgery, it was a lot easier for me. I could talk and eat and breathe without pain and discomfort. And something else had returned that I hadn't felt in years.

I felt more deeply. I saw more clearly.

I remember thinking soon after my surgery that I wished I could bottle up that feeling you get when you have cancer. It's a "Wow, I'm alive, this smells great, look at that amazing color, I can feel my heart beating, we are surrounded by beauty, I love everyone, I'm here now, I have clarity and purpose" sort of feeling.

I've been lucky enough to get to have that amazing, priceless feeling twice in my life so far. That's pretty damn lucky. To face the possibility of death through cancer can be frightening. It can be a wake-up call and provide bursts of clarity. But aren't we all facing death every day? The real challenge of life, I have learned through having cancer twice, is to hold on to the moment as much as possible.

I tried hard to remain present in the moment as much as possible, for as long as possible, but inevitably, it became more and more difficult to hold on to the clarity of purpose I had after each diagnosis of cancer. I think that's okay, in fact. Feeling that intensely is not sustainable.

As a forty-one year old, I have more responsibilities—a career, family, and home. But whenever I have a down moment, I try to center myself and remember that overall feeling I had at the Rose Bowl in 1992 and after my surgery in 2012.

Life is precious; try to enjoy as much of it as you can and stay present. Try to be happy and content. Sure, there will be times when you struggle and things are scary and awful, and it feels like nothing is ever going to get better.

Remember to take comfort in the fact that by surviving, both literally and figuratively, and by struggling and coming through the struggle intact, you will feel more of all the happy moments, more intensely. Sometimes, I think the intensely horrible moments of life are the price we pay for the intensely wonderful moments that follow.

*Erin O'Callaghan, PhD, is the Director and Associate Professor at the California School of Professional Psychology. Her private practice focuses on children and adolescents with depression and chronic illness. Erin can be reached at eocallaghan@alliant.edu.*

---

## A NOTE FROM THE EXPERT: OREL PROTOPOPESCU

Tanaquil "Tanny" Le Clercq (1929-2000), one of the most celebrated ballet dancers of the twentieth century, was a witty, sensuous, and elegant beauty, the only child of a St. Louis debutante and an erudite French-American professor with a drinking problem. Throughout her childhood, her parents' marriage was slowly dissolving. It left behind a bitter aftertaste.

But Tanny was naturally vivacious and fun-loving, as popular offstage as on. An extraordinary dancer, light as an angel, she had a gift for mimicry, word games, and making her friends laugh. Most of them were in the dance world, because Tanny had little time for anything else. Dancing took up so much time that she had stopped going to school at the age of thirteen. By the time she reached her late teens, photographers were featuring her in fashion magazines. She'd become the muse to two geniuses, the most celebrated choreographers of the twentieth century, George Balanchine and Jerome Robbins.

Tanny—thin, exquisite, long-limbed—was the prototype of what came to be known as the *Balanchine ballerina.* She'd been Balanchine's student, but rapidly became a shaper of his taste, a true collaborator. Her way of moving inspired him to create roles for her in which, critics wrote decades later, she had never been equaled.

Jerry Robbins was already famous on Broadway when he came to work with Balanchine's company, the New York City Ballet, in 1949. He'd accepted a drastic pay cut because he'd seen Tanny perform in a Balanchine ballet, *Symphony in C.* The way she let herself go, falling backwards over her partner's arm with astonishing grace and speed, trusting him to support her, was so moving that it brought Robbins to tears. Soon he was in love with the woman as well as the dancer. He proposed marriage, but she chose the much older and much-married Balanchine, who was forty-eight when they wed on New Year's Eve, 1952. Tanny, his fourth and last wife, was twenty-three.

She was at the peak of her career in 1956 when, during a European tour, she came down with what she thought was the flu. The Royal Danish Theatre in Copenhagen was packed with fans, many of them there to see her dance. Tanny could not let her public down, so she performed. The next morning, she could not move her legs. It was not the flu. It was polio.

Days before the tour, Tanny had lined up with other dancers of the New York City Ballet to receive a shot of the new polio vaccine. When first introduced, supplies were scarce, so the vaccine was recommended for the most vulnerable people, those under twenty-five. Tanny, at age twenty-six, was ambivalent. There had been some adverse reactions reported in the press, including paralysis, later traced to a bad batch from one lab. The line moved slowly, giving her time to reconsider. Often sick on planes, she imagined how much worse she'd feel after the shot. Abruptly, she stepped out of line. Tanny told Jacques d'Amboise, a frequent dance partner, that she'd get the shot after the tour.

Now, from her hospital bed in Copenhagen, she tried to make her letters to friends as entertaining as possible. Her mother had to take dictation during the initial, most painful phase of the illness, because Tanny's hands did not function well either. When she was finally able to write by herself, she managed to find comedy in her own helplessness. "I feel like a chicken on a roto-broil now," she told Jerry Robbins, just before Christmas. In the letter, now kept in the Performing Arts Research Collection at the New York Public Library, she wrote, "They say its (sic) bad for people to lie only on their backs, so I keep getting turned around."

After Copenhagen she went to the Warm Springs Foundation in Georgia (Franklin D. Roosevelt's retreat) for therapy. When she came back to New York, her arms and hands had more mobility, but not her legs. Balanchine choreographed exercises for Tanny, clinging to a stubborn faith that he could make her walk again. She stopped believing it was possible long before he did.

For about a decade, Tanny could not bear to be around dancers, except for a few close friends. And yet, she reinvented herself, writing a whimsical children's book in which she personified her cat, Mourka, a naturally talented jumper. In *Mourka, The Autobiography of a Cat*, published in 1964, an orphaned alley cat becomes a famed Balanchine ballerina, trained by the master. Her husband posed with the cat, as did many City Ballet dancers. Mourka seemed as camera-aware as any of them, her paws arched beguilingly over her head. Many of the photographs from the book (by Martha Swope) appeared in *LIFE Magazine*. Tanny had proved that she could be as quick-witted on the page as she'd been on stage.

Next, she collected recipes from her friends and wrote adroit portraits of each one, accompanied by photos (many of which she took herself) for her *Ballet Cookbook*, published in 1967. No trace of bitterness mars her nimble text. She has nothing but praise for the talents of all the dancers who contributed recipes, even the gorgeous young ballerinas who had taken over her signature roles. By the time Balanchine divorced Tanny in 1969, (infatuated with another, younger ballerina), she had found the courage to enter a dance studio again, as a coach.

In 1955, Le Clercq had been the first white ballerina to do a *pas de deux* in a Balanchine ballet with a black partner, Arthur Mitchell, provoking an audible outburst in the City Center audience. A dozen years after that, wheelchair-bound, she became a beloved teacher at the school and company Mitchell founded, the Dance Theatre of Harlem, using her voice and hand signals to convey far more than steps. Today, more than fifty years after her last class, Tanny is remembered by former students as a loving teacher who gave them the individualized attention and expert care they needed to grow.

After her divorce, Tanny chose to live alone for the rest of her life, and she truly lived. She traveled to Europe and the Caribbean, with friends or by herself, but she was never alone for long. Tanny made new friends wherever she went. What had, in part, made her a brilliant dancer—her ability to make the most of each moment—gave her the strength to triumph over the worst fate imaginable for a ballerina. Refusing to let the tragedy of polio define her long, rich life, she focused on enjoying what she had. This was buttressed by her natural capacity for finding joy in the smallest of things.

Balanchine became a friend again. When he was old and dying, Tanny came to see him in the hospital several times. Her marriage had ended, but her deep love for the man and his work had endured. Tanny's wheelchair was often parked in the last rows of the State Theater at Lincoln Center, a building constructed to her ex-husband's specifications. The stage was wide and deep, the floorboards designed to protect the dancers' feet. She had danced on the cramped City Center stage, ten blocks south, far from ideal. Sitting in the dark in the new theater, cavernous as a cathedral, Tanny watched the glorious Balanchine ballets in which she had shone. Now in the audience, she marveled at his inventive genius. Her fingers danced in the air, remembering.

Tanaquil Le Clercq died of pneumonia on December 31, 2000, the anniversary of her marriage to Balanchine. It had been forty-eight years since their wedding day and she had spent most of those years in a wheelchair. "People say I'm brave. I'm not…" she'd said to a friend once. "You have two choices. You can be happy or you can not be happy. I'd rather just try to be happy."

*Orel Protopopescu is an award-winning author and poet, with seven published books for children, teens and adults. She has been a professional storyteller, a writer/producer of educational films, a film researcher/reviewer and an educator, conducting poetry and fiction writing workshops for students and teachers in elementary schools and colleges from New York State to Paris, France. Orel has followed dance for decades, ever since her first ballet lessons as a child. Her biography of Tanaquil Le Clercq is forthcoming. Visit www.orelprotopopescu for the latest information.*

---

This is the moment when you recognize you are happy just as you are. You don't need to wait for some perfect thing—you *are* that perfect thing.

---

## Concrete Action

# Maintain gratitude

From the moment you wake up in the morning until you go to bed, maintain gratitude. There are many ways to do this—but all involve focus and intent. You've learned that you can manipulate your perceptions, and if you find yourself slipping out of gratitude, it's your choice to slip back in. You can actually say "thank you" out loud, or feel free to pray as elaborately as you'd like. The world is your temple—you are your own clergy.

> *"There will soon be no more priests… every man shall be his own priest."*

> —Walt Whitman,
> preface to Leaves of Grass

## This leads me to a final concrete action:

Find your God. Not just any God, YOUR God. The God who gives you peace. The God you can give thanks to and feel something in return.

And if you don't like the name "God"—choose another name. How about Fred?

Find your Fred!

## YOU DID IT

# CONGRADUATION, GRADUATION!

No, there's no typo. I'll explain:

When I graduated from college, I threw myself a graduation party. My friend's relative was a DJ—but the catch was, it was reggae. That was cool, except he didn't have much use for all of the rock 'n' roll records I'd picked out. I remember him chanting over and over, "Congraduation, graduation. Congraduation, graduation." At first I was steamed—I was, after all, an English major, who cherishes grammar—but then I went with it.

This is a good analogy for some of you. I'm sure you found this book annoying at times—okay to read, but a nuisance to do the actual work, perhaps? But then you went with it.

This book is not some medicine you take until you run out of pills, and poof, you're cured! Rather, it's a method you can come back to time after time, to check in and recharge your "happy battery." You can go right to the step you'd like to revisit, or you can do the whole thing over.

You are a student of happy for life. So go with it!

Congraduation, graduation!
Go forth and be happy!

*Love your happy friend,*
*Selene*

## FROM THE DOCTOR'S DESK: LINDSAY S. WEISNER, PSY.D

We want you to sing, dance, read a book, see a play, buy a plant, and remember all the things in life you are lucky to have. Get rid of the people and possessions that clutter your home and your heart. Exercise and eat better and travel and see the love in everything—especially yourself.

But what if all of this isn't enough? How will you know when it is time to seek professional help?

Are you sad or angry or scared more often than you used to be? Has your sleep changed? Have you gained or lost a significant amount of weight? Are your thoughts or feelings interfering with your ability to do your job? Are your reactions greater than most people's reactions would be, if given the same set of circumstances? Have your friends or family noticed a difference in you?

Or, maybe nothing has changed, and that is exactly the problem. Maybe your whole life has been spent trying to figure out why everyone else in the world doesn't seem weighed down by the same fears or sadness or thoughts that you can't seem to stop.

Also, not to be glib, but if you have to ask whether it is time to seek out the help of a professional, you probably already know the answer.

A good way to start the search for a therapist is to contact your primary care physician, OB/GYN, or another doctor you trust to ask them for the name of someone they recommend. You can also contact your insurance company for a list of in-network providers (therapists your insurance company will pay for, with the exception of your co-pay), do a quick search on the internet, or ask a friend. The vast majority of my referrals come from word of mouth. And that's actually how I found my therapist.

**Depression and anxiety can feel crippling. Please remember, if you are thinking about hurting yourself, or killing yourself, or wondering if your loved ones would be better off without you: It is time to seek professional attention from a licensed professional. Call 911 or go to your nearest emergency room immediately.**

I wish you all the happiness you deserve,
Lindsay S. Weisner, Psy.D.
@10stepsfindyourhappy
@PsychShrinkMom

## A Little Help From My Meds

*Full disclosure: Selene and I have been highly conflicted (i.e. politely and impolitely) debating over the decision to include the topic of medication in a self-help book on happiness. We very much believe that with an open mind and willing heart, the book that you are reading can give you the tools to bring the happiness you want—and deserve—into your life.*

*However, just as we include a recommendation to find a (damn good) therapist if you are unhappy and/or anxious more often than not, we also recognize that for some people, medication is the key to clearing away the cobwebs, cotton, or steel walls of depression and/or anxiety that prevent them from being able to get out of bed in the morning.*

*Although I have seen medication help people, I do not believe that medication is for everyone, and I certainly do not believe that medication is a permanent solution.*

*I do believe it is an option worth exploring if the following applies to you:*

1. *Your depression, anxiety, or inattentiveness is interfering with your ability to function at work or with your loved ones at home.*

2. *You are unable to get out of bed in the mornings and/or you find yourself going to bed early at night in an attempt to avoid the world.*

3. *On a daily basis you attempt to numb yourself with food, drink, alcohol, exercise, or drugs.*

4. *You have been feeling this way for more than three months and you are not feeling any better. In fact, you actually feel worse.*

*What follows is an extremely oversimplified explanation on how psychotropic medication works. I say "oversimplified" for two reasons: first, because the unsimplified explanation is tough to understand without a medical degree. Second, because medicine and science are advancing so quickly that the average medical school textbook is updated somewhere between three months and a year and a half. If I were to provide a more exact and detailed explanation of neurotransmitters and medication, odds are pretty good that my explanation would be antiquated by the time this book is in your hands.*

So, how the f@#! do happy pills work?

Some people treat their prescription medication like the Holy Grail of Happiness.

Other people reach for vitamins, adaptogens, and essential oils as they shudder at the thought of putting something "unnatural" in their body.

But very few people understand how happy pills actually work.

In fact, the medications labeled antidepressants—which are used to help both depression and anxiety—support a system in our body that is anything but unnatural.

Sleep, sex, sunshine, and sugary foods all trigger a boost in what I like to think of as "Happy Hormones." You're probably familiar with some of these Happy Hormones, such as serotonin, dopamine, and norepinephrine, but there are a lot more that are lesser-known yet equally mood-improving.

*(It should be noted that some of these so-called hormones are actually neurotransmitters. But, if you know enough about science and medicine that you are aware of this distinction, you probably don't need to read this section—and*

*you're probably gonna hate all the other science stuff I simplify. Yup, move on, don't bother reading, just leave me and my Happy Hormones in ignorant bliss.)*

For *most* people, *most* of the time, the body's supply of Happy Hormones is enough to meet the demands of life.

But, for *some* people, *some* of the time, it's just not enough.

Why?

As we mentioned before, we believe people are like snowflakes—regardless of one's political beliefs. Every person is different, and no physical body is without flaw.

And for some people, the number of Happy Hormones that the body produces are not enough to keep them happy. Even if we were to find a perfect human, there are many real-world problems that decrease the productions of these. Stress, trauma, injury, and insomnia can all negatively affect hormone production.

So, what else *naturally* boosts our *natural* high?

Hugs. (Especially hugs with people you trust and love. Real hugs, not those stiff, awkward Great-Aunt Eleanor Hugs.)

Time with friends and loved ones.

Laughter.

Spicy foods.

Finding a way to enjoy your weekends and vacations—especially if the rest of your life tends to be overwhelmingly rigid and scheduled.

Oh, and one more thing that boosts our natural high in a way that nature intended but cave men couldn't possibly have conceived of: psychopharmaceutical drugs.

The antidepressant medications that are prescribed for anxiety, depression, and pain are simply making more of something that already exists. You know, like when you do squats to build up muscles so that you feel great about how you look in your jeans? Same concept applies here. The hormones, much like your rear end, occur naturally. The medication, much like the squats, just makes a little more of what was already there. And then you feel better.

(Yup, there goes the "medication isn't natural" argument.)

The majority of mood meds work in one of two different ways: Imagine you own a new downtown watering hole, and you are desperately trying to increase revenue. How can we get more people to empty their pockets in exchange for brightly-colored, watered-down, mediocre cocktails?

One option would be to increase the amount of people that come into the bar, since presumably more people means more money. (And more drunk people *always* means more people spending more money.)

Bars will often use a promotion or special event to get more people in the door. For example, a guest DJ or band, celebrity appearance, or half-priced ladies night. More people = more money spent.

Some psychotropic medications work similarly, by allowing more Happy Hormones to come in. More of the *naturally-occurring* Happy Hormones. The medication simply invites more of these Happy Hormones to attend the gathering that is your physical and mental wellbeing.

(See? Still natural, just more of what nature has always created.)

However, there is more than one way to run a successful bar—or live a happy life.

Some bars will advertise that an amazing DJ or band is making an appearance at eleven o'clock, knowing full well that no one will take the stage until well after midnight. Devious? Perhaps. Brilliant? Absolutely.

This strategy prevents people from leaving the bar until the headliner makes an appearance. People stay longer = more money spent.

Some psychotropics work similarly. The medication actually blocks the naturally-occurring Happy Hormones from leaving your bloodstream. This results in a larger amount of good stuff staying where it is supposed to be.

This makes people happier.

Okay. So maybe medication isn't exactly unnatural. But what about other concerns? Weight gain? Sexual dysfunction? Being tethered to one medication for the rest of your life?

The truth is a lot less severe and a lot more tolerable.

Do antidepressants have side effects? Yes, but so does every medication. Antibiotics, Advil, Tylenol, even the over-the-counter vitamins that we purchase at the drug store without thinking twice.

The vast majority of side effects that accompany mood meds are minor and pass quickly. Dry mouth, nausea, and constipation are all usually short-lived and won't interfere with your daily life.

*What about weight gain?* Let's be honest: A lot of us feed our soul by feeding our stomach. And there is a reason the phrase "emotional eating" is so commonly used. We are funny with food when we are feeling like crap. Some people eat too much, some eat too little—but in the end, fat(ter) or skinny(er), you're still left feeling unhappy.

So yeah, some people start meds and begin to gain weight. Some people start meds and lose weight. Does this mean that the medication makes you fat?

Here is what we know: Psychotropic medication does not alter your metabolism. In other words, if you are eating the same amount of food before you start medication that you are eating after you start medication, you will not inexplicably gain a significant amount of weight. There are some medications that may initially cause constipation and/or edema (water retention), but weight gain caused by either would be minimal.

So, does medication cause weight gain?

The real answer: It depends. If you are the kind of person who dives into a pint of ice cream when things go wrong, then when you start medication you may, in fact, lose weight. Since if you start feeling better, you're likely to stop drowning your sorrows in sweets.

If you're the kind of person who stops eating when they are sad or stressed or anxious, then yes, when you start feeling better on medication you may start eating more, and therefore start gaining weight. However, it is also true that some medications may make you hungrier or make you retain more water, and as a result may make you gain weight. In this case, you have to determine what is more important, your pant size or your mental health. There are pros and cons to everything we do in our life. Being happier is a big, big pro.

### *Will medication interfere with my sex life?*

Sex is a huge source of pleasure for some people, and a weekly or monthly obligation for people on the other side of the spectrum. However you feel about sex, it's kinda like chocolate. Once someone tells you that you can't have it, you want it even more.

Some psychotropic medication can have sexual side effects ranging from a decrease in libido to an inability to get aroused (or to get an erection, if you are a man) to difficulty climaxing. A conversation with your prescribing physician about any sexual complications that you fear or experience can usually resolve the issue. Changing your prescription, reducing your dosage, or altering your lifestyle can easily resolve the problem. Also, remember that many of the side effects touted on the label or cited in your Google search are likely to disappear over time.

### *Will I be stuck taking this medication for the rest of my life?*

In all fairness, it depends on what caused your depression or anxiety to rear its ugly head in the first place.

As I stated earlier, some people may have a more constant mood disorder, while many more experience anxiety or sadness related to an emotional disruption in their lives. The death of a loved one, a devastating break-up, a physical ailment, or a life-changing event can all alter our mood or body. But only temporarily.

The best prescribing physicians I know follow the one-year rule: Find a medication that works, establish a dosage that makes the person happier, and after one year, begin to reduce the dosage and attempt life without medication. A lot can change in a year, and therapy and other methods of self-care and self-exploration can reduce or eliminate the need for medication.

Cognitive Behavioral Therapy can help you to change your negative thoughts and the destructive patterns of behavior that often follow. Psychodynamic Therapy can provide you with a greater understanding of what in your past has led you to this point in your present, and how to change what your future will look like.

If you are considering medication and/or would like more information on a specific medication, please contact your primary care physician and/or find a psychiatrist in your area.

Dear Reader,

Thank you for reading this book! I'd love to know your thoughts about it. You can reach me through my website: SeleneCastrovilla.com. I'll write you back!

Please consider writing a review on Amazon, Barnes & Noble, Goodreads and/or anywhere you virtually hang.

I would leave you with the words to a song I learned from the Broadway show *No, No Nanette*, but I don't want to be sued! Look up "I Want to Be Happy" and feel my love. My Aunt Olga played in the orchestra, and I actually knew the actor Jack Gilford (such a sweet man). Hearing him sing in person frequently really sunk the song's message in.

*Here's to happy,*

*Selene*

# FURTHER READING

## Bird by Bird: Some Instructions on Writing and Life
### By Anne Lamott

This is a must for all writers, but I think it's pretty darn good for everyone, as it does have instructions for life. The story the title comes from is a great example.

# Also by Anne Lamott

## Traveling Mercies: Some Thoughts on Faith Plan B: Further Thoughts on Faith

Anne has other nonfiction books, written more recently, which I find have slipped into religion far too deeply for me to read or recommend. But you might like them. Take a look for yourself. She is also a novelist.

## The Secret
### By Rhonda Byrne

I referenced this, and I recommend it! It may not be the first book to give this information about the law of attraction, but it *is* the book that makes it most reader-friendly and easily accessible.

## *What Color is Your Parachute? A Practical Manual for Job-Hunters and Career-Changers*

### By Richard N. Bolles

I referenced this too. Very helpful—and updated yearly.

## *How to Win Friends and Influence People*

### By Dale Carnegie

I've done a lot of library programs, and there are often homeless people in attendance. Sometimes they are disruptive, yelling out gibberish. Such was the case with one homeless un-gentleman, who heckled me and the other author presenting. His words made no sense—until he approached me afterward and pronounced, "You should read *How To Win Friends and Influence People*." So I did. (I try out all advice. Hey, even a stopped clock is right twice a day.) It's good!

## *The Greatest Miracle in the World*

### By Og Mandino

A friend handed this to me at a moment in my life when I was in despair. I read it and followed the "God Memorandum" at the end. Was it written by God? You can decide for yourself. But the lessons in it are important and sound.

Og Mandino has other books too, but I haven't read them.

## *On Writing: A Memoir of the Craft*

### By Stephen King

Another essential book for writers, which is also quite a lesson about "the climb" for everyone else. The story of King's success—and especially how he came up with *Carrie* (and threw her in the garbage)—is amazing and inspirational.

## *Stop Walking on Eggshells: Taking Your Life Back When Someone You Care About Has Borderline Personality Disorder*

**By Paul Mason, MS & Randi Kreger**

If you feel like you're walking on eggshells in any relationship (or if you're walking through an emotional landmine, like I have)—read this book!

## *The Language of Letting Go: Daily Meditations on Codependency*

**By Melody Beattie**

I feel uncomfortable—and confused—by the term "codependency." Nevertheless, I did find this book comforting at a time I needed comfort. It provided daily meditations, which are like mantras. Check out Melody Beattie's books—perhaps they'll appeal to you.

## *The Life-Changing Magic of Tidying Up: The Japanese Art of Decluttering and Organizing*

**By Marie Kondo**

If clutter is your problem, this is supposed to be a fantastic book! (I haven't read it, but many people—including Howard Stern—have.)

## *The War of Art: Break Through the Blocks and Win Your Inner Creative Battles*

**By Steven Pressfield**

This approach doesn't work for me—but many people love it. (Including Sal Governale from *The Howard Stern Show*.) Give it a shot!

## THE FICTIONAL THREE:
### Because we learn the truth from fiction!

### The Catcher in the Rye
**By J.D. Salinger**

This book taught me that I wasn't alone at being alone. Funny, poignant, and heart-wrenching. Everyone should read to understand humanity more.

### A I Lay Dying
**By William Faulkner**

What I said about Salinger…

### Macbeth
**By William Shakespeare**

This play has every human emotion represented in it. My absolute favorite work of literature.

## Four Books For The Ladies:

### He's Just Not That Into You: The No-Excuses Truth to Understanding Guys
**By Greg Behrendt and Liz Tuccillo**

This is a great wake-up call for gals who've spent *so much time* trying to understand *why* he didn't call.

### *It's Called A Breakup Because It's Broken: The Smart Girl's Break Up Buddy*

**By Greg Behrendt and Amiira Ruotola-Behrendt**

Another great book for the ladies, who keep pining for their former man. Some of the lines in here just crack me up, like "Let's play a game. It's called 'Pretend you're not crazy.'" Yes, a breakup can bring on psychoses, for sure!

### *Women Who Love Too Much: When You Keep Wishing and Hoping He'll Change*

**By Robin Norwood**

Yep, this was me, too! If you're giving *all* of yourself—you should read this.

### *Act Like a Lady, Think Like a Man: What Men Really Think about Love, Relationships, Intimacy, and Commitment*

**By Steve Harvey**

What does a comedian/talk show host know about relationship dynamics? A lot! This book is insightful and absolutely worth a read.

## Apologies To The Fellas:

I couldn't find any books specifically for you that seemed strong enough to include. But you can take a look for yourselves!
But if you're the parent of a boy, I highly recommend:

## *Real Boys: Rescuing Our Sons from the Myths of Boyhood*

### By William S. Pollack

How we can help our boys be happy! This book was published when my sons were little, and it gave me the reassurance I needed that I was doing the right thing, even if it was against what society dictated.

# REFERENCES BY SUBJECT

## Accountability

Walker, W. R., Skowronski, J. J., and Thompson, C. P. (2003). Life is pleasant – and memory helps keep it that way! *Review of General Psychology, 7*(2), 203–210.

## Anger

Brescoll, V. L., & Uhlmann, E. L. (2008). Can an angry woman get ahead? Status conferral, gender, and expression of emotion in the workplace. *Psychological science, 19*(3), 268-275.

## Animals

American Veterinary Medical Association. (2012). *U.S. Pet Ownership and Demographics Sourcebook.* Illinois: AVMA.

Anderson, W. P., Reid, C. M., & Jennings, G. L. (1992). Pet ownership and risk factors for cardiovascular disease. *Medical Journal of Australia, 157*(5), 298–301.

Headey, B. (2003). Pet ownership: Good for health? *Medical Journal of Australia, 179,* 460–461.

Kogan, L. & Blazina, C. (Ed.). (2019). *Clinician's Guide to Treating Companion Animal Issues: Addressing Human-Animal Interaction.* Amsterdam: Academic Press. Motooka, M., Koike, H., Yokoyama, T., & Kennedy,

N. L. (2006). Effect of dog-walking on autonomic nervous activity in senior citizens. *Medical Journal of Australia,* 184(2), 60–63.

# Art

Lee, C. J., Andrade, E. B., and Palmer, S. E. (2013). Interpersonal Relationships and Preferences for Mood-Congruency in Aesthetic Experiences. *Journal of Consumer Research, 40*(2), 382-391.

# Art Therapy

Carroll, C. (2014). Feelings in Art. *Arts & Activities, 156*(1).

Emerson, D., & Hopper, E. (2011). *Overcoming trauma through yoga: Reclaiming your body.* California: North Atlantic Books.

Lehrer, P., Woolfolk, R., Wesley, E. (2007). *Principles and practice of stress management.* New York: The Guilford Press.

Malchiodi, C. A. (Ed.). (2012). *Handbook of art therapy* (2nd ed.). New York: The Guilford Press.

Riley, S. (1999). *Contemporary art therapy with adolescents.* London: Jessica Kingley Publishers.

Robins, A. (1987). *The artists as therapist.* London: Jessica Kingsley Publishers.

Van der Kolk, B. (2005). Developmental Trauma Disorder: Towards a rational diagnosis for children with complex trauma histories. *Psychiatric Analysis, 35* (5).

# Creativity

Kaimal, G., Ray, K., & Muniz, J. (2016). Reduction of Cortisol Levels and Participants' Responses Following Art Making. *Art Therapy: Journal of the American Art Therapy Association, 33*(2), 74–80.

Lambert, K. (2010). *Lifting Depression: A neuroscientist's hands-on approach to activating your brain's healing power.* New York City: Basic Books.

Lawrence, E., Rogers, R., and Wadsworth, T. (2015). Happiness and Longevity in the United States. *Social Science and Medicine,* 115–119.

# Dating

Geher, G., Bloodworth, R., Mason, J., Stoaks, C., Downey, H. J., Renstrom, K. L., Romero, J. F. (2005). Motivational underpinnings of romantic partner perceptions: Psychological and physiological evidence. *Journal of Social and Personal Relationships,* 255-281.

Geher, G. (2013). *Evolutionary Psychology 101.* New York City: Springer Publishing Company.

Grammer, K., Fink, B., Møller, A. P., and Thornhill, R. (2003). Darwinian Aesthetics: Sexual selection and the biology of beauty. *Biological Reviews of the Cambridge Philosophical Society,* 385-407.

Rhodes, G. (2006). The evolutionary psychology of facial beauty. *Annual Review of Psychology, 57,* 199-226.

## Emotional Freedom Technique

Guthrie, C. (2019, February) Find Your Pressure Points. *Experience Life,* 28. Retrieved from http://www.experiencelife.com/article/find-your-pressure-points/Levy, J. (2017, November). 5 Emotional Freedom Techniques or EFT Tapping Benefits. *Dr. Axe,* 9. Retrieved from http://draxe.com/emotional-freedom-technique-eft-tapping-therapy/

Miller, B. (2016, June). How To Use Tapping To Solve Any Emotional Or Physical Issue.

*Mindbodygreen.* Retrieved from http://www.mindbodygreen.com/0-25231/how-to-use-tapping-to-solve-any-emotional-or-physical-issue.html

# Exercise

Field, T., Diego, M., and Sanders, C. (2001). Adolescent depression and risk factors.

*Adolescence, 36*(143), 491-8.

Hills, P. & Argyle, M. (1998). Positive moods derived from leisure and their relationship to happiness and personality. *Personality and Individual Differences, 25*(3), 523-535.

Salesi M. & Jowkar B. (2011). Effects of Exercise and Physical Activity on Happiness of Postmenopausal Females. *Sālmand, 6*(2).

# Journaling

Mueller, P. A. & Oppenheimer, D., M. (2014). The Pen is Mightier Than The Keyboard: Advantages of Longhand Over Laptop Note-Taking. *Psychological Science 25*(6), 1159–1168.

# Laughter

Dezecache, G., Dunbar, R. I. M. (2012). Sharing the joke: the size of natural laughter groups. *Evolution and Human Behavior, 3*(6), 775-779.

Dunbar, R. I., Baron, R., Frangou, A., Pearce, E., van Leeuwen, E. J., Stow, J.,… Van Vugt, M. (2012). Social laughter is correlated with an elevated pain threshold. *Proceedings of Biological Science, 279*(1731), 1161-1167.

# Medication

Jeffery, R., Navarro, T., Lokker, C., Haynes, B., Wilczynski, R. L., Farjou, R. (2012). How Current Are Leading Evidence-Based Medical Textbooks? An Analytic Survey of Four Online Textbooks. *Journal of Medicine Internet Research, 14*(6), 175.

# Money and Bills

Kwallek, N. (2007). Color in Office Environments. *Implications, 5*(1), 1-6. Retrieved from http://informedesign.umn.edu/

# Music

Hole, J., Hirsch, M., Ball, E., & Meads, C. (2015). Music as an aid for postoperative recovery in adults: a systematic review and meta-analysis. *Lancet, 386*(10004), 1659-1671.

Lyendo, T. O. (2016). Exploring the effect of sound and music on health in hospital settings: A narrative review. *International Journal of Nursing Studies, 63,* 82-100.

# Purpose

Dunn, E. W., Aknin, L. B. & Norton, M. I. (2008). Spending money on others promotes happiness. *Science, 319*(5870) 1687-1688.

Hooker, S. A., & Masters, K. S. (2016). Purpose in life is associated with physical activity measured by accelerometer. *Journal of Health psychology, 21,* 962-971.

Hooker, S. A., Masters, K. S., & Park, C. L. (2017). A Meaningful Life Is a Healthy Life: A Conceptual Model Linking Meaning and Meaning Salience to Health. *Review of General Psychology.*

Layous, K., Nelson, S. K., Oberle, E., Schonert-Reichl, K. A., & Lyubomirsky, S. (2012).

Kindness counts: prompting prosocial behavior in preadolescents boosts peer acceptance and well-being. *PLoS One, 7*(12), 51380.

Vaillant, G. E. (2012). *Triumphs of Experience: The Men of the Harvard Grant Study.*

Massachuttes: Belknap Press (2012).

# Resiliency

Ginsburg, K. (2014). *Building Resilience in Children and Teens: Giving Kids Roots and Wings. (2). Washington, D.C.:* American Academy of Pediatrics.

# Sex

Muise, A., Schimmack, U., & Impett, E. A. (2015). Sexual Frequency Predicts Greater Well-Being, But More is Not Always Better. *Social Psychological and Personality Science, 7*(4), 295-302.

Komisaruk, B. R., Beyer-Flores, C., & Whipple, B. (2006). *The Science of Orgasm.* Maryland: John Hopkins Press.

Rinklieb, C. E. (2006). *Women's Sexualities: Generations of Women Share Intimate Secrets of Sexual Self-Acceptance.* New York City: Read File Publishing Co.

Assari, S., Moghani, L. M., Ahmadi, K., & Kazemi, S. D. (2014) Association between Sexual Function and Marital Relationship in Patients with Ischemic Heart Disease. *The Journal of Tehran University Heart Center, 9*(3), 124-131.

Flynn, T. J., & Gow, A. J. (2015) Examining associations between sexual behaviours and quality of life in older adults. *Age and Ageing, 44*(5), 823–828.

# Theater

Catterall, J. S., Chapleau, R., & Iwanaga, J. (1999) Chapter in E. Fiske (Ed.), Champions of Change: The Impact of the Arts on Learning. *Involvement in the arts and human development: General Involvement and Intensive Involvement in Music and Theatre Arts,* 1-18. Washington DC: Arts Education Partnership and President's Committee on the Arts and Humanities.

Dunbar, R. I. M., Teasdale, B., Thompson, J., Budelmann, F., Duncan, S., van Emde Boas, E., & Maguire, L. (2016). Emotional arousal when watching drama increases pain threshold and social bonding. *Royal Society Open Science Publishing, 3*(9).

Walker, S. R. (2014). It's not all just child's play: A Psychological study on the potential benefits of theater programming with children. *Honors College,* 198.

Meeks, S., Vandenbroucke, R. J. & Shryock, S. K. (2018). Psychological benefits of attending the theatre associated with positive affect and well-being for subscribers over age 60. *Aging Mental Health,* 1-8.

Essays, UK. (2018, November). Effects of Theatre Arts on Emotional Intelligence. Retrieved from https://www.ukessays.com/essays/psychology/effects-of-theatre-arts-on-emotional-intelligence-psychology-essay.php?vref=1

Slusser, D. C. (2008). Relationship Between High School Theater Participation And The Development of Workplace Competencies. *Electronic Theses and Dissertations,* 258.

# BOOKS BY SELENE CASTROVILLA

*Luna Rising*

*Melt (Book One in the Rough Romance Trilogy)*

*Signs of Life (Book Two in the Rough Romance Trilogy)*

*The Girl Next Door*

*Saved By the Music*

*Seeking Freedom: Ending Slavery in America*

*Revolutionary Friends*

*Revolutionary Rogues*

*By the Sword*

*Upon Secrecy*

**Selene is pleased to have a piece included
in the charitable book anthology**

Travel in the Sixties*, whose proceeds fund art
and music therapy for Alzheimer's patients.*

**For more information about Selene and her books,
please visit her website:**

**SeleneCastrovilla.com**

# ABOUT THE AUTHOR

As a child, Selene Castrovilla was thrown down a well and spent decades clawing her way out—metaphorically. Overcoming circumstances the likes of which have emotionally decimated others, she became an award-winning, multi-published author and a nurturing mother. She's travelled extensively for book signings and appearances, sharing her thoughts on life and happiness along the way. After years of being told her wisdom changes lives, and at the prompting of her older son Michael, she's mapped her steps to happy for you!

Selene holds an M.F.A. in Creative Writing from The New School and a B.A. in English from New York University.

You can learn about what makes Selene happy on her website, selenecastrovilla.com. (One of these "things" is her younger son, Casey, who she can't bear to leave out here!) Join Selene's mailing list for periodic happy boosts!

She is represented by the Ethan Ellenberg Literary Agency.

# ABOUT THE AUTHOR

Lindsay S. Weisner, Psy.D, is a wife, mother, psychologist, writer, and (regretful) PTA volunteer. She received her undergraduate degree from Georgetown University and her Doctorate from Long Island University.

Dr. Weisner has wanted to be a writer since she was seven years old, when she painstakingly—and painfully—typed her first novel on a blue and white typewriter. The dramatic plot involved time travel, Madonna, and Raggedy Ann.

Since then, her writing has improved slightly, and in 2014 she won the Cosmopolitan Magazine Fiction Writing Contest. Her fiction is represented by Jessica Alvarez at BookEnds Literary Agency (www.bookendsliterary.com).

Dr. Weisner owns and operates a successful private practice in Long Island, where she specializes in treating teenagers and adults with anxiety and relationship issues.

Dr. Weisner can be reached at drlindsayweisner@gmail.com or through her Facebook page, Mental Wellness Consultants @ Long Island Psychologists.